The Reunion Planner

The Step-by-Step Guide
Designed to Make Your Reunion a Social and
Financial Success!

Fourth Edition

Linda Johnson Hoffman
Neal Barnett

Goodman Lauren Publishing   Los Angeles, California

Requests for such permissions should be referred to
Publisher: Goodman Lauren Publishing
www.reunionplanner.com
info@reunionplanner.com

Hoffman, Linda Johnson.
The reunion planner : the step-by-step guide designed
to make your reunion a social and financial success! /
Linda Johnson Hoffman, Neal Barnett. -- Fourth edition,
revised & expanded.
pages cm
Includes index.
LCCN 2014907898
ISBN 978-0-9-747265-8-8

1. Class reunions--Planning. 2. Class reunions--
Handbooks, manuals, etc. 3. Reunions--Planning.
I. Barnett, Neal. II. Title.

LB3618.H64 2014   371.8'9
                            QBI13-600302

Thank you to my reunion planning team: Neal, Connie and Leslie, for your years of partnership and friendship. Also, to my high school friends and committee members who have worked with me on our reunions, thank you for your continued support and friendship and for inspiring this book so that others can learn from our great experiences.

- Linda Johnson Hoffman

To my wife Wendy, my children Jeff and Lindsay, and my parents, sisters, and extended family – with whom I always look forward to reuniting.

- Neal Barnett

Contents

Quick Guide to Software Tips

Introduction

It's time for a reunion! Whether it's a class, family, university, sorority or fraternity, corporate, military, or any other group being reunited, as reunion organizers, we hope to make it a spectacular event. While we're at it, let's imagine an event that exceeded all expectations.

Sound like ambitious goals? With a little organization and forethought, along with a few enthusiastic volunteers, these goals are attainable and well worth our time and effort.

Of course, those of us who plan reunions realize it takes energy, and lots of it. Frankly, it represents a labor of love. To be successful, reunions must be: 1) a memorable experience, 2) raise enough resources to cover all expenses, and 3) retain a surplus for the next reunion. Our primary goals are to bring people together to reminisce, reestablish friendships, and to value the reunion that rekindled these relationships. This book will help realize these objectives.

As the title suggests, this book was designed to help make your reunion a social and financial success. While people who go to their reunions have different expectations, they all want to have a good time. To that end, it will take more than providing a basic package. At the same time, it's important not to lose money! Any recipe for success calls for planning, organization, cash flow, and enthusiasm. If the passion is there, we can help with the rest. The result will be a fun-filled, personalized reunion that is well-attended and financially successful.

Reunions are Part of our Culture

As we get older, we become more nostalgic and have a greater interest in revisiting the past. Reunion research shows that more than 350,000 class and family reunions are held annually. Military reunions are less common, but the incentives and interest in having them might be even stronger.

Using the Companion Software Application

Planning a reunion is a unique and gratifying experience, and yes, it is also time consuming. However, it will be well worth all the effort when it's over and guests leave with wonderful memories and revived connections. While this book is designed to help simplify and streamline the reunion planner's efforts, the companion software was developed to realize these goals more efficiently. Just having the software for the organization and efficiency it provides is enough of an incentive to plan the reunion.

If a computer is not accessible, ask someone who has one to help, the convenience it provides is well worth it. Listed below are three areas that identify how the software categorizes the event information.

Organization

- Categorize all the details of the group's reunion including names, addresses, phone numbers, and email addresses
- Location status
- Response status
- Payments and items purchased
- Biographical information
- Add additional guests per group
- Checklists and to-do lists for each step of the way
- Name tags, with or without photos
- Import data from prior reunions

Reports

- Samples of memory books, invitations and to do lists
- Statistical data on group attendance and location
- Create class roster of names, phones numbers, and other **contact** information for a memory book or other hand out

Actions

- Print mailing labels, envelopes, name tags with pictures
- Send emails, with attachments or pictures
- Create estimated and actual budgets
- List vendor information
- Print document samples of invitations, mailings, reservation forms, questionnaires, and memory book pages

Small computer icons as shown here are referenced throughout this book whenever usage of the software is recommended.

New in the Fourth Edition

Reunion planning has become much more web-based with the ease and efficiency of announcing the reunion, dispersing information, finding people on the internet, and communicating via email and other social media. In accessing the Internet, this book will help with shortcuts and tips on finding venues, making payments, shopping for vendors, and purchasing souvenirs and gifts.

This edition also has fresh ideas on centerpieces; invitations name tags, displays as well as activities, games, and door prizes.

To help make the reunion even more profitable, set up a free reunion website on **http://reunionplanner.com**. With such instant accessibility and information now available, the goal of producing a reunion that is a financial and social success is only a few steps away.

How to Use This Book

The Reunion Planner is meant to be a tool for reunion committees to create the most successful event possible. Based on trial and error and feedback from other readers, this section has tips on how this guide can be the most useful.

The Contents outline each chapter, and along with the Index, is a useful reference tool. Organized by a chronology of tasks, each chapter describes a step-by-step process up to the reunion event and beyond. The Appendix has sample invitations and a budget worksheet. *Do not despair if there is not enough of the recommended time to plan the reunion.* Decide what can be accomplished in the time available. Conversely, if too much is undertaken, things may get done carelessly.

Overall Approach

Focus on the sections of this book that apply to your reunion, and follow these suggestions:

- Scan through the entire book first. While ideas start flowing, it will help to have an initial overview.
- Keep a highlighter and Post-It-Notes® handy. Highlight those pages and ideas you wish to refer to later.
- Jot down ideas and questions on a notepad and bring them up at future reunion committee meetings. Transfer successful ideas to a task list.
- Reference the book throughout the planning process. Be sure to concentrate on the relevant time frames.
- Use the book and companion software together. Once the data is in the computer, countless hours will be saved in printing lists, exporting and sorting data, generating mailing labels and name tags, keeping a budget, and much more.
- Review any **Quick Tips** that are peppered throughout the book.

- Get copies of the book to committee members. In this manner, everyone can contribute to a more successful event.
- Refer to our website, **http://reunionplanner.com**, for the most current information, ideas, tips, and feedback from other users. We encourage participation by asking questions, offering advice, and sharing experiences. It's a win-win situation.

Review the chapter outlines below. Highlight those areas that most reflect your reunion plan. Chapter 1, **Get Started**, offers reasons to plan one's own reunion. Alternatively, if the committee just doesn't have the resources to do it and professional planners are hired, this chapter will suggest how to work with paid organizers and still maintain a personalized reunion. **The Reunion Planner Checklist** that follows is a handy reminder of all conceivable tasks. Copy these pages, or go to our website, **http://reunionplanner.com**, and download the list for free to keep a record of items as they're completed.

Chapter 2, **Organize Effectively**, describes how to *Strategize, Structure, and Streamline* while coordinating an event. It includes ideas for raising seed money, arranging a committee, event timing, and maximizing efficiency.

Chapter 3, **Find the Right Location,** offers assistance in finding the perfect location for your reunion.

Chapter 4, **Locate People,** talks about how to find people, especially on the Internet. Websites are cited that offer the most comprehensive value as of this writing. Considering how quickly the information superhighway changes, the only way to keep pace with the latest offerings is to continue checking the Internet, including our website and others for the latest updates.

Create a money plan using the worksheet in Chapter 5, **Create a Budget.** Crucial to any successful event is maintaining accurate accounting records. Included are ideas for raising funds and how to decide on a ticket price so expenses are covered and a profit is realized. There are also tips on last minute fundraising.

Chapter 6, **Build a Foundation**, provides guidance on announcing the reunion with thoughts on ice breakers, activities, entertainment options, videography, and photography unique to reunions. Accounting guidelines complete this section.

Chapter 7, **Design an Ambiance,** *is* comprised of ideas for themes, souvenirs, memory albums, and name tags.

Chapter 8, **Encourage Attendance**, presents tips on how to increase attendance at the reunion. One of the more wearisome aspects of planning a reunion is encountering reluctance. As organizers, we put so much effort into planning the event that it's discouraging to come across disinterest or negativity. This chapter offers suggestions for soothing some of the more common perceived fears and anxieties.

Reunion Decor is reviewed in Chapter 9. Topics include decorations, displays, and memorabilia along with advice on what items to sell at reunions.

Chapter 10 provides **Family Reunion Basics** while Chapter 11 has *Military Reunion Strategies*, each with targeted ideas for locations, games and activities, souvenirs, awards and fundraising.

Chapter 12, **Countdown**, contains program and award strategies. Chapter 13, **Final Arrangements**, examines how to organize an effective registration process.

Chapter 14, **Reunion Day,** sketches out events over a weekend reunion. Chapter 15, **Wrap Up,** helps with closing costs and responsibilities. Finally, Chapter 16, **After the Reunion,** has suggestions for keeping connected between reunions.

This book focuses on "in the flesh" reunions. The premise for holding reunions is to spend time together to reconnect, renew, and reminisce. This is not possible solely on the Internet. Electronic reunions can't take the place of being together in person, in a celebratory manner over an extended period of time. Humanity disintegrates once physical connections disappear. Then we simply become digital robots. What an unpleasant path that would be.

1. Get Started

Reunions! Creating them or simply attending them triggers many emotions in each of us. They can invoke happy memories, nostalgic reflections, and a desire to rekindle relationships with those we shared important life experiences with. Reunions can also evoke squeamishness from those who did not have the most wonderful of pasts.

As mentioned earlier, it is a precious few who are willing to take on the challenge of planning such events. Just by reading this book, you are one of the dedicated folk that care enough to want a spectacular event. There may still be some doubts that you have the time, assistance, and resources to make it work. However, since you are in possession of this book, you have already made the first commitment and are well on the way toward creating a fabulous reunion.

During high school, I was secretary of my senior class. I never thought about reunions back then, nor did I think it was my responsibility to organize them. However, nine years after graduation, recognizing that someone had to start the process if a reunion was going to occur, I took the initiative. Having put on our 40 year high school reunion, the core group was intact, and we began the journey.

Why Take the Initiative

It represents time, energy, and money just to get to a reunion. Expectations naturally run high. It's a big responsibility to take on and there is a lot to live up to. Nevertheless, by the time you finish this chapter, if you are not thoroughly convinced you're ready to take the plunge, consider hiring a professional reunion planner. Once one reunion is under your belt, the basics will be in place for the next one. If it helps, remember that you can reduce involvement later, but someone needs to initiate the process. After a committee is formed, an infectious enthusiasm takes over.

Finding Time within a Busy Schedule

Once the plan is in motion, time and energy would be best served by initiating the following procedures:

- Organize an effective reunion committee, one with energy and that works well together
- Plan and prioritize the tasks
- Take advantage of this reunion "how to" book for shortcuts, ideas, and guidelines
- Try to keep egos out of the way and incorporate the talents and energies of other committee members
- Use committee meetings and reunion projects as opportunities for enhancing your organizational abilities, writing talents, and time management skills
- Use the Internet and the latest technologies to save time and effort

10 Top Reasons to Plan a Reunion

1. People look forward to reunions, and they will be very grateful for all the effort put forth on their behalf.
2. The event will be personal.
3. Reestablish friendships. You have the opportunity to reconnect at length with friends and family members from by-gone days, more so than only attending a reunion.

4. Enjoy the camaraderie of working with a committee toward a common goal. Cementing friendships is a distinct bonus.
5. Enjoy mini-reunions during committee meetings. You'll find yourself immersed in conversations with former classmates or family members whom you haven't spoken to in a long time.
6. Receive tremendous gratification knowing you've brought people together who might otherwise never have seen each other again.
7. Seize the opportunity to put together a genealogy chart, family history, or other permanent record you always wished you had.
8. Provide networking opportunities for family and friends.
9. Gain self-esteem and satisfaction upon completion of this milestone event.
10. Savor the memories for years to come.

Bonus. Guests are more likely to respond positively to a phone call or email from a classmate, family member, or friend who is contacting them.

Hiring Professional Planners May be Worth Considering

Family reunions are generally smaller and can be handled by family members. However, successful class reunions are usually larger and therefore require many phone calls and other time-consuming tasks. It's better to have a reunion organized by professional planners than not to have a reunion.

What follows is a chart that outlines some of the typical reasons alumni often hire professional planners for high school reunions. The adjacent column shows how alumni can handle those same tasks on their own. Hopefully, these points will help with the final decision.

Professional Planners	Plan it Yourself
Up Front Costs	
Initial expenses for room deposits, website design, and other costs are covered.	<ul><li>Collect advance ticket money from members of your committee.</li><li>Plan a small fund raiser before your reunion.</li><li>Ask if you can pay deposits in installments as you collect money. Most businesses will work with you.</li></ul>
Locating People	
Many in-house resources for locating and contacting people.	<ul><li>Use Facebook, Google, and other free search sites.</li><li>Phone calls from classmates and relatives will get better responses.</li><li>You get to keep the updated information.</li></ul>
Getting the Word Out	
Postage is covered for all mailings.	<ul><li>Email is free and quick.</li><li>Create a reunion website and direct guests there to find information, get updates, and pay for their tickets.</li><li>With 5-10 people, snail mail can be stuffed, stamped, and addressed in no time.</li></ul>
Event Registration	
Registration and greeters at the reunion is staffed by the professionals.	<ul><li>Ask alumni spouses, family members, or friends to handle check-in. They get to meet and interact with guests.</li><li>Organize short shifts. People will be glad to take turns.</li><li>The committee gets to keep any profits.</li></ul>

If you find you are just not able to devote the time to such a project right now, but you definitely want a reunion to happen, hire a professional reunion planner. Even when working with professional planners, this book will help result in a more successful reunion. Stay as active in the planning as time allows. Form your own committee. Authorize the contents of all mailings. It is also a good idea to oversee mailings and other reunion items.

The National Association of Reunion Managers (NARM) is a non-profit organization of professional reunion planners. Their members must follow strict industry standards with regard to contracts and communications with alumni committees and high schools. Register your reunion on their website and find a professional planner among their members in your area. Their website address is: **http://reunions.com**.

Always make absolutely sure the organization or professional you hire has good references. We know many hard-working professional planners who plan fabulous reunions, but we've also seen professional planners disappear right before the reunion, taking thousands of dollars of reunion ticket revenue with them. Therefore, we offer the following guidelines in engaging anyone.

Get References
- Check comments posted on various websites.
- Call the high school to get names of companies that have organized successful reunions for other classes.
- Check with the alumni association or other class committees for their recommendations.

Do Due-Diligence
- Meet with them. Ask to see photos of other reunions they have organized.
- Look at their portfolio, sample mailings, name tags, and photo albums. Ask to attend a reunion they are currently planning. This will really help to visualize your event.
- Check out their insurance liability carrier and verify that their policies are current.

A Contract with Professional Planners should include *Your* Conditions

When you are ready to sign a contract, be sure it reflects your interests and includes the following conditions:

- Secure a bond (like an escrow account) payable to the class committee or create a joint account. Should the company fail to perform, the committee could lose a lot of money, time, and effort.

- The committee is to be given copies of any alumni lists the professional planner has developed, including names and contact information. (Updates might not be easy to obtain from them, since herein lies the basis for securing your future business.)

- Be sure to get all alumni responses (read them yourself) from the Missing Persons list as well as the returned, filled out questionnaires. This way you can follow up on leads the professionals might not pursue.

- You must be allowed to contribute and have final approval on the design and content of mailings and other related items. The professionals usually include your alumni or committee names to legitimatize their efforts in correspondence, so your input on all reunion materials is necessary.

- If none of the locations they offer are desirable, find your own destination. Be aware of the fact that reunion companies have prior deals with certain venues, caterers, entertainment, and photographers. You may have better luck and even get a better rate with your own choices.

- The committee will be given the complementary overnight room offered by most hotels to groups holding large events there.

- Name tags must include yearbook pictures! (If their "package" does not include this essential memento, insist on it or have them refund a portion of each ticket price. Then make your own. Like we said, in our experience, pictures are essential.)
- After the reunion, the professional photographer must send the photo proofs directly to your committee. (This guarantees your possession of the reunion pictures should the organizers not follow through with this final task.)
- Stay closely involved in all aspects of decision-making, including the selection of table centerpieces, door prizes, and souvenirs. Your ideas will result in a more personalized event.

There are many good professional planners in the marketplace, but you have to stay alert. While they may sell themselves as the answer to all your worries, consider that, for them to be profitable, they have to juggle several reunions at once. Their highest priority might not be you and yours. Shop around and hire a professional you feel truly understands your vision.

Whether you plan your own reunion or hire professional planners, get started right away! The sooner, the better! Once the first meeting happens and everyone is excited and bursting with anticipation, you will know the best decision was made.

Reunions: Important Life Milestones

Planning reunions can be very satisfying. Besides the opportunity to reconnect, revisit, and renew relationships, you get to know more about those you shared an important part of your lives with. You will be heartened by how you all survived.

A former teacher who attended a high school reunion put into perspective much of what reunions have come to represent.

"Many of you have attended not only high school together, but junior high, and sometimes even grammar school. In your transition from childhood to adolescence, you shared many experiences both painful and triumphant and in many ways left an indelible imprint on each other.

A reunion is a celebration of life; not just your life, but the lives of all those around you. It offers you an opportunity to revisit a period of your past that had so much influence in guiding you to become who you are today. It is an affirmation of your successful transition from youth to maturity, and the good news is, you have survived. Many of these people share that triumph with you tonight. These are such infrequent yet important opportunities in your lives. Thank you for letting me share this moment with you tonight. I encourage you to attend all your school reunions."

In Summary, Four Key Points

1. Get Adequate Assistance
The total number of volunteers who really pitch in can determine the success of the event. The more people who are available to search for and find former classmates, family, and friends, the higher turnout you can expect. A continual flow of ideas and enthusiasm, plus clear lines of communication make the process move along smoothly and the job becomes more fun than work.

2. Plan and Prioritize
Set priorities and goals. Such a structure is essential to any successful endeavor. Being able to set up an organizational plan, manage a budget, and provide follow through on tasks are keys to success.

The more time volunteers commit to it, the more successful the reunion will be. Organizing the time and resources for this project is the first step. Time management is the foundation of good organization, so it is essential to take the time to plan and prioritize this event. Research indicates that every hour of planning saves three or more hours.

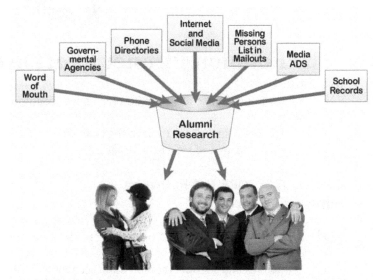

The Elements of Effective Reunion Organization

3. Follow a Checklist
The *Checklist* that immediately follows this chapter is a handy reminder of all conceivable tasks. Circle the ones that pertain to you. Make several copies of this list, highlight specific tasks, and distribute to each volunteer. This way, each person has his or her own to-do list and can check off the items as they're completed.

4. Use Reunion Planner Software
Having the group's information organized into a computerized database will make the process much easier. The time-saving techniques alone will be worth the cost. By keeping all the data organized in such a fashion, the wheel won't have to be reinvented for each reunion.

The Reunion Planner Checklist

Get Started
- Set up committee, collect seed money, begin people search
- Decide when and where to have the reunion
- Set up a budget and select the ticket price

ONE YEAR BEFORE THE REUNION
Organize Effectively
- Form the Committee
- Decide when and where to have the reunion
- Create reunion website
- Set up files and set up a reunion bank account
- Begin the search for people
- Create a budget

NINE MONTHS BEFORE THE REUNION
Build a Foundation
- Get the word out
- Send out the first mailing
- Select entertainment and photographer
- Organize activities and games
- Plan multiple events

Design the Ambiance
- Choose mementos, souvenirs, and name tags
- Consider possible social action project
- Hire videographer
- Invite special guests

Encourage Attendance
- Meet regularly to make phone calls
- Prepare and send second mailing

SIX MONTHS BEFORE THE REUNION
Reunion Decor
- Plan decorations, displays, and centerpieces
- Organize special presentations or honors
- Order t-shirts, banner, and other mementos
- Decide and arrange for awards and door prizes

THREE MONTHS BEFORE THE REUNION
Countdown
- Update address list, edit histories, continue phone calls
- If required, get event insurance
- Update reunion website, Facebook, and other media
- Create or order name badges or buttons
- Create or order table centerpieces
- Prepare signs and door prize coupons
- Prepare any presentations or announcements
- Prepare printed program
- Get reunion booklet or other handout ready for print
- Update guest roster and attendee list
- Make and order name tags as reservations come in
- Update reunion website, Facebook, and other media
- Select preliminary award winners

TWO WEEKS BEFORE THE REUNION
Final Arrangements
- If appropriate, mail or email tickets
- Confirm delivery logistics with the entertainer, videographer, photographer, and other suppliers
- Verify attendance and make accommodations, if necessary, for invited guests
- Finalize program announcements and award winners
- Verify delivery of donated door prizes
- Proof memory album draft or other handouts
- Submit artwork to printer

ONE WEEK BEFORE THE REUNION
Loose Ends
- Prepare final list of paid attendees
- Prepare registration packets for pre-paid and will call
- Make signs for registration area
- Give meal count to caterer and required payment to venue
- Verify room set up and equipment arrangements with the banquet manager

THE REUNION EVENT
Reunion Day
- Bring reunion day checklist, program notes, announcements, awards, prizes, raffle tickets, etc.
- Remind committee members of their tasks
- Enjoy the event
- Clean up and retrieve supplies at end of reunion

Wrap Up
- Complete and proof read photo book, deliver to photographer
- Send memory albums and other hand-outs to those who paid but did not attend the reunion events
- Send out any additional items that people purchased
- Send thank you notes
- Update reunion website with photos, comments, and notices
- Send any donations to school, association, or charity
- Close bank account once all checks have cleared. Move any remaining funds to savings account
- Store reunion supplies in convenient location

Aftermath
- Keep the ambiance alive by maintaining regular contact
- Hold follow up committee meeting to discuss reunion successes and pitfalls

One Year before the Reunion

1%

2. Organize Effectively

The basis for an organizational approach to event planning can be summed up in three words: *Strategize, Structure, and Streamline.* Following the techniques described in this chapter will pay for itself with the enjoyment everyone at the reunion will experience and the financial and emotional benefits that are gained. Insufficient planning will result in a so-so event.

Strategize: Form the Committee
The Reunion Committee
Form an effective committee to begin planning the event. Start this at least one year in advance. While there usually are one or two people in any group who initiate a reunion plan, it is recommended that a committee be formed for assistance in all other aspects of planning.

In most groups, one person usually emerges who has the willingness and capability to lead. This person will typically chair the reunion committee and oversee all the tasks. However, to prevent burn-out and maintain sanity, one person shouldn't be burdened with all the responsibility. It is most effective if tasks are delegated and the labor is divided.

Reunion Committee Assistance

- ✓ It is probably easiest if one person is in charge of entering all the reunion data into the software program.
- ✓ Make regular data backups

Be prepared if some members come to committee meetings only to socialize and reminisce. The leader must be assertive to help everyone stay on track. Assign very specific tasks during the meetings. This is good practice and helpful for everyone involved. There are several tasks that committee members can handle:

Reunion Committee Task Checklist
- Search for people
- Maintain the main address list or database
- Prepare mailers, announcements, and other notifications
- Edit the alumni or family histories for a memory album
- Help design a memory album and/or photo book
- Research entertainment
- Plan activities and/or games
- Organize a secondary reunion event as an early ice-breaker, following-day picnic, family outing, high school tour, etc.
- Help plan a fundraiser
- Prepare a ceremony honoring special guests
- Update reunion website with current information and pictures
- Prepare a survey for inclusion in the memory album
- Manage ongoing public media announcements
- Prepare pictures, slide show, and/or video
- Prepare a Memorial Board or poster
- Arrange for door prizes
- Order a banner
- Find and order t-shirts or other items for the group
- Prepare registration packets
- Solicit advertisements for a business directory
- Set up a memorabilia table
- Create and organize table centerpieces
- Select room decorations and displays
- Prepare a hand out of the reunion program
- Order souvenirs
- Coordinate a charitable donation

Committee Structure

The group energy of a committee is what maintains an infectious enthusiasm. In building a committee, choose those people who have the time, talent, and a genuine interest in making the reunion work. Those who work well together and have good follow through are essential.

In establishing meeting times, a regular meeting time, such as once a month, is a good way to keep the momentum going and committee members can plan accordingly. If an in-person meeting is not required for a particular month, consider using free online chat formats like **Skype** or "**Facebook Video Chat.**" This allows more members who live out of town to attend meetings. A lot can be accomplished during a few in-person gatherings geared toward collecting seed money, conducting the people search, and handling any mailings or electronic notices. Someone's office will be very handy since everyone can go to a phone to make calls and be in one place to compare results. If there are more volunteers than phones, delegate other tasks to those who don't want to make calls.

Volunteers can also call and search the internet from home. If phone lists are given to people to take home, make sure to select people who are trustworthy to follow through and return the results to the person responsible for updating the primary list.

To maximize results and reduce the burden on one person, ask for enough assistance. One or two people will likely emerge as the leaders and take responsibility for important tasks. The one or two committee members who surface as the leaders should be in charge of the software database containing all the reunion member data. With a task checklist, like the one shown before, or a computerized printout (described later in the chapter), it will be easier to identify and assign specific tasks. If deadlines are instituted, one of the leaders should follow-up on seeing if tasks are being completed.

Assign Tasks and Due Dates for Committee Members
- ✓ Under To-Do Lists, print lists for each person with their assignment, the date given, and the due date.
- ✓ Mark dates when completed.

Utilize everyone's skills in areas they excel at or have a strong interest in. The main focus at the first meeting should be on accomplishing two goals, collecting seed money and organizing the search for people. Reserve all other tasks mentioned above to subsequent meetings.

Raising Seed Money

Since there will be postage, phone, and stationery costs, as well as deposits on the hotel and entertainment, the committee is going to need some initial financing.

- The easiest and quickest method is to ask committee members to pay for their tickets up-front or to lend money to the reunion bank account.

- Offer deadlines for early ticket purchases, including discounts or payment installments. This will require meticulous bookkeeping, but will effectively cover the initial costs.

- Arrange an early fundraising event that won't require much work. Hold it at an inexpensive restaurant, committee members' home, or other venue. Charge a small fee above the event cost. This should also stimulate interest on the upcoming reunion.

- Order t-shirts or other mementos with your family or class name and charge an amount over the cost. There are many t-shirt vendors that offer lower rates for large quantities. These make great souvenirs. ClassB has an array of t-shirts for any occasion. **http://classb.com**.

- Organize a pot luck meal, chili cook-off, or dessert party in a committee member's home, a park, or at a community center. Charge a per person fee, offer discounts to children, and encourage family attendance.

- Charge a fee for advertising business cards in your mailers and on the reunion website. This is a win-win situation. It is an easy fundraiser and is an inexpensive advertising vehicle to a predisposed receptive audience.

- Attract corporate and community sponsorships. Solicit local businesses that might have a connection or affinity toward your group. Offer them advertising incentives.

- Promote an early auction in reunion notices or on the reunion webpage. Offer at least 10 items, such as the free hotel room at the reunion event. Ask hotels, stores, services, professional sports venues, and restaurants to help sponsor your event. The highest bidders win. It's also good advertising for participating companies.

- Save money on initial printing costs by requesting in-kind donations in lieu of ticket payments. For example, a committee member may have a print shop that can provide free or discounted printing services for stationery, name tags, mailings, or personalized tickets.

Committee Meeting Essentials

After the initial committee meeting, set sequential meeting dates before people leave. Send reminder emails or notices about the date, place, and time, and include an agenda (see sample below) so members know what to expect and can plan their schedules accordingly and bring any appropriate materials.

Beverly Hills HS Reunion Committee Meeting
Sunday, October 13, 2013
Bill Jones' Office, 10:00 a.m. About 2 hours

Agenda
–Assemble first mailer
–Collect ticket money for hotel deposit

Structure: The Reunion Framework
The basic structure is determined by deciding when and where to have the reunion. Send out a questionnaire to gather input from your invitees on preferences for dates and locations. Venues are booked at least a year in advance, so 18 months to two years is an appropriate lead time to send out a questionnaire.

When to Have the Reunion
The exact date for a reunion will be determined by the chosen location's availability. Class reunions are typically planned during the summer months: June through September. Nevertheless, don't feel limited; if winter or spring turns out to be more convenient for the majority of attendees, choose the most desirable date. Thanksgiving, for example, is a good opportunity for class or family reunions since many are close to their homesteads around this time of year.

Summer dates enable families to plan vacations around school breaks. Year-end holidays or three-day weekends are ideal times for family reunions. Some resorts, airlines, and hotels may have reduced rates during off-seasons.

While a theme party may not be typical, it offers a variation on the routine. Plan the reunion around a holiday, a nostalgic occasion, special family birthday, anniversary, or other commemorative event such as homecoming weekend for high schools, colleges, or universities. Alumni from sororities and fraternities regularly plan such annual events. (See Appendix for sample sorority homecoming weekend invitation.) Many combine the event with a fundraiser for the House or charity they sponsor.

Theme Ideas
- A "dress-as-you-were then" party

- Holiday-of-the-month theme: St. Patrick's Day, Fourth of July, Halloween, Thanksgiving, New Year's Eve, etc.

- A historical or time period theme such as a commemorative event or day, a wedding anniversary, an elder family member's birthday, a graduation, or release from military service

- Be different! Have fun! Choose an unusual theme that has significance for your guests to dress up accordingly: country western, all black and white, disco, rock and roll, carnival, ragtime, Caribbean, a luau, masquerade, or Roaring 20s. Use this as a focal point for planning food and decorations. Hotels might even have accessories and backdrops to rent.

- Center the reunion on a related special event such as a museum opening, school dedication, ship commissioning, or religious occasion.

If you're from a small town or had a small graduating class or military unit, or were in a sorority or fraternity, consider having an all group event where overlapping years are included. This accommodates friendships across or between a broader range of ages.

Quite often, schools organize an event based on an anniversary of their existence. This is a good opportunity to combine an extra event with the schools' Sunday barbeque or picnic.

Streamline: Time and Effort Saving Techniques
Streamline the time and effort involved by utilizing the tips, tricks and shortcuts, learned the hard way by other reunion planners. This book will also demonstrate how to computerize guest information and quickly categorize all your data and how to use the internet for fast efficient ways to locate people. The software that was designed along with this book will help organize the information carefully. All areas of reunion planning benefit from this tool.

The Reunion Planner ® Software

This book demonstrates how the companion software application (if purchased as a package) can be an invaluable tool and save hours of planning. The best part is that the wheel doesn't need to be reinvented for each reunion. All the information is in one location, easily retrievable and simple to update; a major convenience in our busy lifestyles.

How the Software Program is Designed

For example, when searching for people and entering guest information, the following lists help organize your data.

- All Invited Guests
- All Attending
- Not Attending
- Located
- Not Located
- Deceased
- Address Confirmed
- Responded
- Not Responded
- Out of Towners
- Tickets Paid
- Purchased Items
- Fully Paid
- Partially Paid
- Not Paid

Create lists under each of these headings. Keep careful records and print copies of all names, addresses, and phone numbers. Reports can be viewed either alphabetically (using women's maiden and married names) or by area code.

Mailings are made much easier because our program prints hundreds of address labels in just a few minutes using any listing mentioned above or for individually selected names. Email messages to your group in mass or small groups of names, and if necessary, include any attachments.

If there are guests traveling from long distances, check the *Out-of-Towners* box in the "Alumni Information Screen" for labels and reports relevant to them. This function is helpful in notifying guests of special group travel packages and discounts.

The *Located* report is helpful whenever trying to contact those whose whereabouts are already known. The *Not Located* report is good for printing out the list of persons still needed to be found for committee calling sessions and may contain their last known information. This report can also be used as the Missing Persons List for mailings and flyers.

Check the *Confirmed* box when the address information has been verified and the person wants further information on the reunion. It is useful when making initial calls to verify their information. It is different from the *Located* box because while someone's address is known, they may not be able to attend this reunion. This way the committee saves time and money by not reaching out to them again for this reunion.

The *Responded* box indicates they have replied yay or nay to the current reunion.

The *Deceased* box is helpful for preparing a list of names for the memorial board poster.

There are also boxes to designate *Faculty* or *Committee Member* and the *Grad Year*, which is helpful for school reunions that combine classes for multi-year reunions.

Keep track of attendance statistics to see the percentage of guests invited, located, and responded. The software breaks the information down according to total, male and female attendees.

The software is also helpful in assembling handouts like a memory book or photo album that may include a roster with names and contact information.

Budget Assistance

To feel totally confident you won't run out of money, set up a detailed budget. The software has an *Estimated and Actual Budget* function for making calculations based on the existing and anticipated financial situations. Test different ticket prices based on various expense scenarios.

- Estimated expenses
- Estimated receipts
- Anticipated net balance

Other Features

- Use the *Comment* section to enter RSVPs and interest level. This is very useful for future phone drives.
- Print invitations
- Make name tags with pictures and corresponding guest names
- Use *Bio Page* with multiple text fields
- Assign seating assignments, table numbers, and meal choices
- Export reports into PDF, Word, Excel, and Text formats
- Create fields for items to purchase as t-shirts and sweatshirts with size options

3. Find the Right Location

The Reunion Venue

An original estimate determines the site selection and affects every other decision. For a larger estimated attendance, choose a place accustomed to dealing with groups your size.

Hotels with large banquet facilities are the most popular and the most ideal places to hold reunions since everything is already on the premises. If the selection is a venue that doesn't serve food, factor in the costs of hiring an outside caterer. In computing costs, add rentals of tables, chairs, linens, and other needed items.

The primary consideration to bear in mind in making these initial choices is to create a comfortable environment that is conducive for people to feel relaxed enough to reconnect. Everything else is secondary. It doesn't have to be an expensive dinner-dance! Whatever is selected, base the decision on how much the budget allows. Preparing a preliminary budget is extremely helpful. (Review Chapter 5, *Create a Budget*, before making a final decision on where to hold the reunion.)

When shopping for prospective places in which to hold the reunion, bring a list of questions (see below). Besides price, the selection will be based upon the look and size of the meeting rooms, nearby lodging, restaurants, convenience of location, parking ease, the size of the reception area, and the overall "feel" of the surroundings. The following list will help identify potential reunion locations.

Questions for the Catering Manager

1. **Look at all the available rooms**. Do any have the right ambiance for your group? Are there outdoor facilities, smaller meeting rooms? Is it spacious enough? Too spacious? Are windows important? Where can a dance floor be set up?

2. **Menu**. Check selections and prices. Are there service options for buffet or food stations as opposed to the usual sit-down dinner? What is the total price per person, including tax and tip?

3. **Deposit.** If the deposit requirement is higher than your current cash flow can accommodate, can the deposit be paid in installments?

4. **Cancellation procedures.** How much are you liable for in the event that your reunion gets canceled?

5. **Reception area.** Is there a separation between the reception area and the dining room? If not, see if the venue has lattices or other room dividers for these areas. A separate reception area is a big plus as it allows for a smooth check-in process.

6. **Timing.** Are there any restrictions, rules, and/or time limitations for setting up the room(s)? Is there a time limit for how late you can have loud music? What is the quitting time for bartenders, servers, cleanup crew? Do they offer and can you pay for extended hours if necessary?

7. **Liquor costs**. What are the drink prices? Can you bring in your own liquor? Is there a minimum for bar sales, and how much is charged if the minimum is not met?

8. **Meal overage.** What percentage above the guaranteed meal count is allowable for unexpected guests? Are there food choices available for people on restricted diets?

9. **Photo area**. Is there a clear and spacious area for the photographer to accommodate potentially long lines for the individual pictures?

10. **(Non-hotel/restaurant sites) vendors.** Do they use specific vendors and caterers?

11. **Additional costs.** Are dance floors, reception tables, chairs, and storage facilities considered "extras?" If so, what are the fees?
12. **Accessories.** Can a podium, bulletin board, sign posts, and easels be provided?
13. **Smoking.** What is the smoking policy?
14. **Accessibility.** Where are the accessible entrances?
15. **Decorations.** Can your staff hang a banner? Where? Can posters or other displays go on walls?
16. **Electrical outlets.** Are there sufficient electrical outlets and power to accommodate any equipment brought in?
17. **Sound system and audio visual equipment.** Are computer monitors and microphones provided? If not, can you bring your own and will there be a staff person to oversee the equipment?
18. **Child friendly needs.** Highchairs and booster seats?
19. **Video or slide show.** Is a projector and screen available? If so, how much does it cost? If not, can we bring our own and will a staff person be able to oversee the process?
20. **Room (hotels only).** Is a free guestroom and/or hospitality suite offered with the event?
21. **Room (non-hotel).** What nearby accommodations are available?
22. **Final count.** When is the final head count and payment due?
23. **Umbrellas, hats, and coats.** Hat and coat check-in?
24. **Security guards.** Are there parking lot guards or security guards patrolling the area during the reunion?
25. **Parking.** Valet, self, or free parking? If so, what is the cost?

Other factors besides cost that determine a reunion location:
- Proximity to a school or other nostalgic area
- Largest concentration of family members
- Proximity to an airport
- Ease of accessibility

- Appropriate activities or facilities nearby, such as restaurants, tourist attractions, entertainment venues, or hospitals

Once the location has been determined, reserve it promptly. If the event is being held in May or June, remember that these months are popular for weddings, proms, and graduation parties, and are scooped up far in advance.

That said; don't make a hasty decision either. Even though you don't want to chance losing the perfect place, don't be forced into making a quick decision. Location managers want your business as much as you want to book a location. Place a temporary hold on the room while looking at other sites. Once the venue is selected, remember to notify any other sites that you asked to be held.

Before signing on the dotted line, make sure all the verbal conditions, such as price, deposit dates, and services along with complimentary rooms and other "extras" agreed upon, are in writing. If you feel it warranted, you can have a lawyer look it over first. Perhaps someone in your committee knows a lawyer that can donate some time.

We highly recommend a visit to a similar event being held at the chosen location. This will provide invaluable insight on how your event will appear and perhaps avoid any pitfalls. You might also get some decorating ideas.

Negotiating Points
Some prices might be negotiable once you're definitely interested. It usually works better to seem as though you're still shopping. Explain that you are a volunteer or on a non-profit committee, and you might be able to get their non-profit rate. If you have a record of what was spent on your last reunion and the number of rooms that were reserved, you will be better prepared to negotiate.

Ask for reduced rates on parking too. Compare the benefits before the deal is negotiated. If you don't ask, you won't get.

Location Ideas

There are countless venues that are suitable for reunions. The choice may be decided by the type of reunion being planned. For example, hotels with banquet facilities are good for high school and military reunions while campgrounds might be ideal for a family reunion. Of course, there are other considerations involved in choosing the right location including your group's needs. A variety of ideas are listed below.

Hotels

These are obvious first choices since they have convenient ball rooms and banquet facilities. These establishments usually have group rates for the ballroom, overnight rooms, and meals. Use your reservation to negotiate for a hospitality suite, extra tables and chairs, bulletin boards, and any audio/visual equipment.

Another advantage to having your reunion at a hotel is the free overnight room or hospitality suite usually provided to groups holding major events there. Hotels may also offer a free overnight room per a certain block of reserved rooms, usually 20-40. The committee can use the complimentary room to coordinate the flow of the event and to change clothes.

For Guests Staying Overnight at a Hotel

Reduced overnight room rates are the custom for large groups holding events in their venue. It is all negotiable, so if you can convince them your group will bring in at least 20 rooms, you will get a better rate. Hotels typically block out rooms at a discounted rate by a certain date without a financial commitment from your group. After that date, the going rate kicks back in. Be sure to mention this booking deadline in all reunion correspondence.

Quick Tip: Welcome guests staying overnight with a courtesy gift such as a basket filled with a small snack, the reunion itinerary, and a memento. As the event nears, ask the hotel for a list of your group's registered guests to determine the number of baskets needed.

Restaurants and Country Clubs
These venues will have many of the same amenities as hotels. However, it will be necessary to find convenient lodging for out of town guests and others who may want to spend the night close to the reunion. Try to negotiate a group discount rate at nearby hotels, motels, or bed and breakfasts for guests who require overnight accommodations. Restaurants may offer more meal options at better prices than hotels. Be sure to check prices and sample some menu options before making a final decision.

You may be able to arrange free shuttle service to and from the reunion site if enough rooms are reserved. Again, the advantage of these locations is that food and other requisites are included in the per-person meal charge.

Dinner Theaters, Clubs, and Theme Parks
Many theme parks (e.g. Disneyland, Sea World, Disney World, and Universal Studios) and dinner theaters have "party packages" that include lists of entertainers, video specialists, etc.

Museums, Art Galleries, Mansions, and Estates
This idea offers a welcome alternative to the typical ballroom location and may provide an extra incentive to attend. Since food, refreshments, servers, tables and chairs, dance floor, and event insurance must be brought in, costs are higher than locations that have everything on their premises. However, it may be worth it to have a really fun venue. Chambers of Commerce should have a list of mansions, estates, or designer showcase homes rentable for one night events.

Museums and galleries often offer their premises for large events and may have a list of recommended bartenders and/or caterers. Compare prices of the on-site caterer with your own. Get references from any caterer with whom you are not familiar. Ask for a sample tasting.

Resorts, Parks, Campgrounds, and Historical Sites
These destinations are great opportunities for folks to reunite for several days in a casual setting. In addition to room and board, retreats offer various organized activities. Resorts like Montecito Sequoia, in the Northern California Sierra Mountains, is a beautiful location surrounded by wilderness and lakes and has activities for all ages, including games, hikes, water skiing, archery, tennis, evening concerts, or just the indulgence of relaxing among the trees.

If planning a one-day event in a local or national park, a spacious area with picnic tables and barbecue facilities would be ideal. Picnic areas and baseball diamonds in city-operated parks should be reserved early as they are often already booked far in advance.

Sea Voyage, Yachts, and Cruise Ships
A reunion during an ocean voyage, a day in a marina or lake, or a few days cruising along a river or up and down a coast line could be a refreshing alternative to the typical ballroom dinner-dance. Contact a travel agent and check the rates on cruises or call some larger cruise liners directly: Princess Cruises, Royal Caribbean Cruise Lines, Holland America, Hornblower Cruises & Events, and others for their group travel packages. An interesting and helpful website, **http://cruisecomplete.com** is set up for travel agents to compete in finding the best destination, ship, and prices for a cruise vacation. They help select cruises, plan port visits, and plan formal onboard reunion activities. A cruise offers activities for all ages and activity levels.

Houseboats

A reunion on a houseboat cruising down a slow, calm river or lake might be a lot of fun. While houseboat rentals are more popular during the summer months, June - September, better deals can be had during off-peak times. Some of the more popular lakes are California Delta, Lake Don Pedro, and Trinity Lake in California; Lake Mead and Lake Mohave in Nevada; Lake Lanier in Georgia; Lake of the Ozarks in Missouri; and Lakes Meredith and Amistad in Texas. Depending upon the time of year and the size of the boat, the rental prices vary.

A 59-foot boat, for example, at Pleasure Cove on Lake Berryessa in Napa County, California, for the off-peak month of October has a current daily rate of $697 plus tax. They also have nearby wine tours or offer a houseboat wine-tasting package on the Lake, currently at $1,741 plus tax based on occupancy of up to 10 people for two nights on a luxury 60ft Eagle houseboat. Effectively, that's an average of $94 per person per night. For more prices and availability, contact: **http://foreverresorts.com** or call 1-800-255-5561.

The Hiawatha Beach Resort & Houseboat in Walker, Minnesota, **http://hiawathabeach.com**, currently offers rates of $1,515 for either a four-day mid-week or a three-day weekend reservation. These two sites also offer military and AARP discounts.

School Gym, Field, or Hall

Consider holding a class reunion right at the high school. The school may allow use of their outdoor grounds, hall, or gymnasium at little or no cost to alumni. Rent a jukebox. Guests could come dressed in specific-era attire. You may have to purchase additional one-time event liability insurance in addition to what the location already covers. Do this as an inexpensive interim five-year reunion. Serving alcohol may not be allowed on school premises. However, if it is a daytime event, food, water, and soft drinks may be all that's needed. Look for a location near the school or military base that has catering facilities for alternative events.

Families and other reunion groups may also consider using such facilities but may incur additional fees if the group doesn't have a connection to such venues. Use any negotiating skills available if this seems to be the best location for your group.

Camps, Conference Centers, Lodges, and National Parks
A camp or lodge in a woodsy atmosphere makes for a relaxing and inexpensive reunion. Nature is very conducive to real connecting. Plan a day-long outing or a weekend retreat. Arrange activities around meals and evening gatherings being sure to allow ample free time so guests have quality time together at their leisure. Make sure whatever location is selected meets your groups' needs and has nearby markets for additional meals and snacks.

We reiterate—popular locations need to be reserved well in advance, as long as two years prior! Universities, private conference centers, national parks, lodges, camps, and youth hostels all have the necessary facilities. Club associations, visitor bureaus, and conference centers all have many offerings and services for groups.

An inexpensive way to house members of a group is to make use of college campuses. During times when school is not in session, especially during the summer months, universities offer an affordable alternative to hotels. A nationwide broker for the campuses helps meeting planners find suitable meeting spaces and lodging in empty college dorm rooms. Perfect for family reunions looking for low-cost lodging and meeting rooms with access to caterers, nearby restaurants, and activities. Visit **http://campusconferencesolutions.com**

Frontier Reunions
Dude ranches, former army forts, historic towns, ranchos, or old homesteads can be a unique setting for family or military reunions. Many offer camping, lodging, sporting facilities, biking and hiking trails, tours, site-seeing, horseback and stagecoach rides, fishing and hunting, educational and cultural activities, and

restaurants. There typically are docent-led tours, games, and activities for all ages. Convention and visitor bureaus will have more information on such rental locations.

Wineries and Vineyards

There are now wineries in all 50 states, so planning a family or other type of reunion in a vineyard can be a clever incentive to encourage attendance, especially if your group enjoys good wine. Explore vineyards that have accommodations for hosting large groups inside or outside their facilities. Wine tasting at a vineyard could also be a fun day activity for smaller groups. Check out the local inns and hotels for group discounted rates in any of the nearby regions. Several wineries have event packages. In Napa Valley, California, for example, **Andretti Winery** offers both indoor and outdoor venues for groups ranging from 10 to 250 people. Contact their Special Events Department at 888.460.8463 ext.229, or email them directly at **events@andrettiwinery.com.**

Alternatively, a fun day activity for adults who don't want to drink and drive is to reserve a van for small groups with door to door pickup and drop off. A typical seven hour tour is led by knowledgeable guides who will work with the group to choose a few of the many wineries to visit. Call 707.257.1950 or visit **http://wineshuttle.com.**

More Opportunities

Travel sections in newspapers often have articles, special deals, and group discounts. Check the off-season rates. Search online under "Cruises" or "Marinas" and comparison shop. Also, see if your destination city or county has a Visitor Center and Convention Bureau. Their websites are wonderful resources for finding out about the region you will be visiting with contact information on nearby recreational facilities, sporting venues and activities, family friendly attractions, historical sites, scenic drives and tours, shopping, full service hotels, and other highlights of the area. Most websites also have a calendar of events throughout the year to assist you in developing your schedule. Each bureau will have a dedicated group sales manager to answer any questions or to provide assistance.

There are many more ideas, books, and websites to explore for additional ideas on reunion locations, products, and services. You are only limited by your imagination.

Multiple Day Combination of Events
Holding several events over a weekend or a few days allows everyone more time and multiple environments to reconnect. It also offers different opportunities for people with scheduling conflicts or financial constraints to attend at least one of the gatherings.

The Menu
Food is generally not uppermost on most people's mind when deciding whether or not to attend a reunion. However, we all look forward to the main occasion and less than wonderful food can make a substantial dent in the overall success of the event.

Select a menu that is in sync with the ambiance being planned. The sit-down dinner is the classic scenario. Guests are usually given two or three entree choices. However, a sit-down dinner confines guests to one small table talking to 2 or 3 people for a good part of the evening. A buffet style dinner or food stations afford greater meal variety and guests can mingle more. To avoid long delays waiting in line, suggest the caterer set up the buffet table so that people can utilize two sides.

In choosing a menu, add the appropriate sales tax and gratuity when determining the total cost per person.

Per Person Cost:

Dinner:	$50.00
Sales tax @ 8%:	4.00
Gratuity @ 18%:	9.72
Total Cost:	$63.72

Of course, the total cost per person must include all other reunion expenses. Costs can be reduced by serving appetizers, finger foods, and dessert and by supplying your own liquor and soft drink bar. Selling alcoholic drinks will require obtaining a liquor license for the day (if the location doesn't already have one) and hiring professional bartenders. Check with your states' alcoholic beverage control department for appropriate procedures. If providing a bar, sell drink tickets so the bartender doesn't have to handle money. Call some restaurants and hotels for ideas on types and amounts of liquor to have on hand based on the estimated attendance. Alternatively, search for a party drink calculator online, as there are many.

After a menu is selected, organize a field trip committee meeting at the venue for a meal tasting and sample the selections your group is leaning toward.

Event Ice Breakers

Many different emotions come into play in anticipation of attending any reunion. Planning a casual pre-reunion get-together on the Friday night prior to the main event is a comfortable way to relax and begin reminiscing. A Sunday brunch, picnic, or sporting activity is another casual setting that won't necessarily incur additional costs, especially if it is a potluck.

Ice breakers can be orchestrated, casually planned, or presented as an impromptu function. A Friday night pre-reunion gathering that wouldn't involve much effort could be in the hospitality suite or cocktail lounge at the hotel sponsoring the main event. Alternatively, if the reunion is being staged at a restaurant or other similar venue, there might be a nearby hotel that can accommodate smaller groups in their bar area for the pre-mixer.

Perhaps someone on the committee can handle a small gathering in their home or garden where guests can bring their own drinks and snacks. By extending the reunion, these smaller events give out-of-towners and those with scheduling issues more time to visit.

4. Locate People

Beginning the Search

Some people never bother to find out about reunions and hope someone will find and contact them. As hard as it is to find people, and as much as people do want to attend, many of us fail to make that simple phone call to their alma mater, school, family member, or military base to find out if a reunion is being planned. Then, we're thrilled when someone finds us!

Finding and notifying people represents a large part of planning a reunion because it takes the most time and effort, but it can also be the most rewarding. Sleuthing may be tedious, but the rewards of finding and reconnecting with people you've been searching for is inherently gratifying. Catching up with people by phone provides a personal connection that wouldn't occur by email or letter. By reaching out to them, it demonstrates that they are remembered and their presence is desired.

According to research, the greatest percentage of people still reside within 50 miles of where they grew up. A good starting point is searching on the internet. You will have a distinct advantage in locating people if you know the first, middle initial, and last names, age range, and/or a relative's name.

The internet is the most convenient resource for finding almost anything. It has made the task of finding people and announcing reunions easier, quicker, and broader in scope since you can get instantaneous information and access to phone directories all over the world. Along with Facebook pages, and similar social networking vehicles, new websites are appearing daily, as schools, military organizations, religious groups, and community associations all have websites. In fact, people locator sites are some of the most popular sites on the internet.

Organize the Search

If you have a large list of names, begin by dividing the phone lists among all committee members into groups. *Request that updated addresses retrieved from everyone's search be legible!* Remind callers to ask for the whereabouts of other potential reunion guests during telephone conversations. Offer to reimburse volunteers for home-originated, long-distance charges. You can also distribute phone lists by the area codes they live in.

Committee Phone Meeting Lists

- ✓ If volunteers are making calls from home, print out phone lists by area code.
- ✓ If calls are being made at one location, print out the entire phone list and divide it evenly among available callers.

The Old Stomping Grounds

For class reunions, visit the school. It serves as the central headquarters, which is an important link for alumni information. While there, take pictures, get any existing alumni lists, etc. You never know what other useful materials and information might materialize.

Usually high schools and colleges have faculty members or coordinators to handle reunion inquiries. Meet with this person. By making an appearance, you may ensure that the staff is familiar with your group's reunion.

Some things to look for:
- Graduation list
- Diploma list
- Enrollment cards
- Any information with dates of birth, military unit, or rank
- Alumni lists
- Professional or alumni associations

- Documents with the first names of both parents. (Parents are less likely to have moved.)

An Alumni Association may have helpful information, such as email addresses or phone numbers, from their Membership roster. Also, there may be contact names from other classes that could be knowledgeable about accessing class lists of possible siblings of your classmates.

Tour the grounds of the school, hometown, church, or former military base. Get pictures of the area as it looked at the time and take photos of how it looks now. Aligning before and after photos next to each other are fun poster displays at the reunion or in mailings and newsletters and help to create a nostalgic feeling.

Check the school's student store, Chambers of Commerce, local historical society, or military base for possible items to be raffled off, displayed, or used as door prizes or souvenirs for the reunion. There may be old newspaper articles, newsletters, song sheets, yearbooks, or other useful memorabilia. With an added reunion caption or logo, create t-shirts, sweatshirts, hats, glassware, or pens to sell at the reunion. Here's what one planner found at her high school:

> *"The student store had stuffed animal replicas of our school mascot which I bought for table centerpieces. A greater find was their last copy of our senior yearbook. Knowing it would be in high demand by alumni who had since lost their, I bought it and auctioned it off at our reunion."*

Continue the Contact throughout the Year
This "home base" is an important link for people who have been out of touch. To facilitate this conduit and prevent any potential misinformation, periodically contact the school or alumni association, for example:

- Send flyers with the reunion information
- Call the school periodically to verify that information being distributed about the reunion is correct! Administrative staff and the reunion details could get lost in the process.
- Add the organization in any reunion email blasts
- Ask to post reunion announcements on their website or in a newsletter

Suggest the School Help Too!

There are a few things a school can do to help this process along and create good will at the same time. It would be clever, forward thinking for the high school reunion coordinator or alumni association to prepare a reunion packet for each graduating class. The packet or electronic device should contain the names, parent's names, addresses, and phone numbers of graduating seniors with one copy kept at the school and another given to a class officer (who usually are the ones initiating reunions). What a wonderful gift to the class! Not only would this establish an alumni list for future reunion committees, it also creates fundraising potential for the school. If you are organizing a class reunion, pass this suggestion along to your high school and tell them to spread the word among other schools.

What Happens if the School No Longer Exists?

You are at a distinct disadvantage if the school no longer exists or if address records have been lost or destroyed. If a class list can't be located, try other methods. First, check if there is an alumni association. Even when schools close down, alumni associations have been known to continue for many years and maintain records. Only a few names might be for your class, but at least some addresses may be current. Without an institution, there are other options.

Many reunions have been planned based solely on the names and pictures in the yearbook. This actually is a great starting point for the first phone drive. Bring the yearbook to each committee meeting. It is also an excellent reference when making calls.

If someone has the original commencement program it will, at a minimum, provide a list of names.

Internet Resources

Check to see if the group being reunited has a website. Online directories are frequently updated, some more than others. Try several search engines to maximize results. Use all the free search devices that are discussed in this chapter before paying for any online assistance.

When searching these sites and finding that there are twenty Bill Smiths to contact, don't get discouraged. The last one may be the one you are seeking. As for all those wrong numbers, if the person answering understands the reason for the call, he or she will likely be more receptive.

Free People Finding Websites

Currently, the availability of free "people finding" websites are few and far between. As of this writing, we have identified only a few websites providing free address and phone number information. Websites either advertise their services on the free sites or furtively place their links on the site hoping users will pay for any detailed information. Be careful when searching on the free search sites only to be taken to a paid section, hoping to peak your interest. Exhaust the free sites before paying for information.

The sites **http://zabasearch.com** and **http://whitepages.com** are still helpful and are free people finding resources. However, most people searching sites now only give limited information for free and charge fees to acquire any significant details. Facebook is a great resource for finding people as more people continue to sign up with their own profile. It is especially helpful since many female members include their maiden names. The site **http://search.yahoo.com** will find anyone who has any public record by listing several websites where the name might exist. Also, just by "Googling" (i.e. typing the individual's name in the search bar on Google), a number of alternative websites and listings will direct you to more people finding websites. Remember that this worldwide resource can usually find anyone, anywhere since privacy is practically nonexistent on the internet.

Class Reunion Websites

For the most part, every public and private high school, college, and university has alumni associations and websites with listings of whom to contact for information.

There are many websites that list upcoming reunion information and contain alumni names for class reunions. Gradfinder, **http://gradfinder.com,** for example, has free alumni lists if you sign up on their site. "For American students who attended high schools overseas, there is an organization for military brats (offspring of the U.S. military stationed overseas) called "Overseas Brats." This organization is dedicated to preserving the heritage and experiences of students and educators of American families stationed overseas. You can take a look their website by heading to **http://overseasbrats.com/AlumniReunions.asp** *to find out more.*

While there are many other potential websites to list reunion announcements, our advice is to list your reunion on the most well respected and free sites and then direct your alumni to the reunion website created by your committee.

Make sure someone on your committee is responsible and able to keep the site current and interesting. Update it regularly and maintain it even after the reunion. Then, when the next reunion is just a year away, the site will be available early on and still be easily accessibility.

Our latest venture at **http://reunionplanner.com** is to provide planners free and secure customer-focused websites for their reunions. Other websites charge monthly fees for maintenance, but we offer planners and their invitees and attendees an easy and efficient location to post reunion information, add pictures and videos, blog with alumni and friends, and sell tickets. We also have resources and products to help enhance the reunion event.

Military Search Websites

There are many military reunion sites on the web, but we are listing the most used and respected sites at the time of this publication.

Military Brats Online (**http://militarybrats.net**) is set up to help reconnect with the U.S. Military Brats heritage and friends. Register for free and look for alumni whether you attended stateside or overseas schools. Also, search for old and new friends, create blogs, and participate in the community including contacting other members. Members can form their own discussion groups, chat, blog, and create photo albums and events.

VietVet (**http://vietvet.org**) has a Lost and Found locator for Vietnam veterans and friends of vets looking for each other. Anyone can post searches. The Vietnam Veterans home page lists veterans' groups and a place to post searches. It announces unit reunions, prints newsletters, and lists points of contacts. The Vietnam Veterans' memorial wall page can be accessed at: **http://thewall-usa.com**. It lists veterans killed in the war here.

The Veterans History Project (**http://www.loc.gov/vets/vets-registry.html**) of the American Folk life Center collects, preserves, and makes accessible the personal accounts of American war veterans for posterity. The Veterans History Project database (formerly National Registry of Service) is searchable by veterans' names, branches of service, wars, service units, service locations, medals, rank, and interviewer and donor names. Display screens provide service history information as well as basic material descriptions.

Look for any current armed service personnel through one of the military sites and home pages for each branch of the military service. Add your own listing in the branch with which you are associated. Locators are categorized by the names of wars and branch of service including World War I, 1914-1918, World War II, 1939-1945, Korean War, 1950-1953, Vietnam War, 1961-1975, Persian Gulf War 1991, and Afghanistan and Iraq Wars, 2001-present.

The Korean War Project (**http://koreanwar.org**) is the home page for Korean War veterans. While it does not have listings for veterans who are still living, it has a casualty list of veterans, killed or missing in action. The site also has a list of reunions.

Family Finding Websites

The Church of Jesus Christ of Latter-day Saints (LDS) is by far the largest and most comprehensive resource in the world for researching family histories, genealogical research, and family trees. See their website at **http://lds.org**. Their well-known Family History Library in Salt Lake City, Utah, is connected to their Family History Centers (FHC) in each state and throughout the world. Each has a collection of databases that lists millions of names of people who have had previous research done, and anyone can access this information free. All these sites have links to, and information on, similar search engines and topics. Check out the related websites they suggest. For example, **https://familysearch.org/search** is an excellent site with ancestral files that are quite extensive.

Ancestry.com contains a variety of databases (online public records) including immigration, military, census, court and/or probate deeds, land and vital records (birth, marriage, death, etc.) that are perfect for preparing family trees. You can perform an ancestral global search for relatives still living even though you might only know a few details on the person you're trying to find. For those who have passed on, you can look through the Social Security Death Index from 1935 to the current date. You need their full name and date of birth and date of death. However, some of the originally-free information is now available via paid subscription only.

Geneaology.com has been around awhile. It helps you trace your family's history with how-to articles, genealogy classes, and other resources. It has ideas and a search engine that goes through available public records, but you have to register with the site and pay membership fees depending on what link on the site is used.

Many families have established their own Internet sites with genealogy pages and ongoing family reunion information and communications. Look at these sites for ideas on starting your own internet family resource center.

Reunions Magazine (**http://reunionsmag.com**) specializes in all reunions and will announce any military, family, or class reunion on their website and in their quarterly magazine.

People Finding Sites by Profession
Martindale.com helps you find anyone whoever practiced law in the United States. Just provide a name in their "People" section on their search link.

The home page for the American Medical Association is available at **http://ama-assn.org**. Under "Doctor Finder," search by physician name or medical specialty. You must include the state. It will give the doctor's full name, state, city and zip code, whether they're an AMA member or not.

Free General People Finding Sites
- **Facebook.com - Find Friends**
- **Switchboard.com**
- **Whitepages.com**
- **Zabasearch.com**

Non-Internet based People Finding Resources

- Request referrals during the phone drives
- Post and send "Missing Persons List" on reunion website along with periodic mailings
- Use parents' addresses; if you're lucky enough to have parents' first names, that's even better
- Local newspapers and radio stations often offer free public service announcements about reunions
- Church bulletins, alumni association newsletters, genealogy society newsletters, or military magazines usually have a section listing upcoming reunions
- County Assessor's Office. There is probably a fee to search public county property tax records. However, if a realtor is on the committee, they can research property tax records for free.
- University alumni records and college associations, such as sororities and fraternities
- Reunion committees of bordering class years might have relatives of people you are looking for

In all likelihood, the fastest and most economical method for finding people is through the internet. Nevertheless, you only have so much time to commit to these efforts. The core of reunion planning should be on making personal phone calls to get people excited about attending the reunion.

For updates on new people-finding sites, visit our website at **http://reunionplanner.com.** Planners also have the ability to create their own reunion website. Various reunion products and services are offered to help make your reunion planning a bit easier and, of course, help you design the event not to be missed.

5. Create a Budget

It is always good practice to set up a budget to ensure the financial success of any event. For a reunion, it is not only good practice, it is essential for selecting a ticket price and determining the kind of event you can afford.

Set a Goal

Estimate the preliminary cost projections using the Budget Worksheet. This worksheet will help create a preliminary budget. Make several copies of this page, and use a pencil, as you will likely be making changes. Once you have a figure for an expected turn out, experiment with different ticket prices that will accommodate the estimated expenses. Closer to the date of the reunion, a final budget should be prepared. After the event, a closeout budget must be completed to verify your estimates and financial records. A final, actual budget will be very helpful for the next reunion.

Prepare an Estimated and Actual Budget

- ✓ Under Budget Data, enter assumptions and prepare an estimated budget.
- ✓ Move the cursor to Actual Budget and enter correct amounts as expenses are incurred.

Assumptions

Total Guests

In setting up a budget for school reunions, as shown in the sample below in the assumptions section, enter the total class size. For other reunions, estimate the total number of people in the group's membership.

Estimated Turnout

Be conservative. In determining the expected attendance, a slight underestimation of guests is a safer bet for choosing what size banquet room to book. A restaurant or hotel can always add a few more tables if more people show up, but a large room with few tables is . . . well, not very cozy. Various factors will affect attendance, such as the time between reunions. The more frequently-held reunions will generally experience less attendance.

For more assistance, contact other reunion coordinators. Catering Managers at large hotels or restaurants will be helpful too. Experience is always a reliable resource. In the sample budget below, for a 20-year reunion, the total group membership was multiplied by 40%. This included spouses.

A per-unit estimated turnout will be required for deciding how many individual items are needed. Use this figure when only one item, such as T-shirts, programs, or photo books, per classmate or family unit is necessary. It is safe to assume, for example, that each family will share one cookbook. In the sample budget below, 65% of the total estimated turnout, 130, was estimated.

ESTIMATED ASSUMPTIONS	
Total Group Membership	500
Estimated Turnout @ 40%	200
Estimated Family Unit (each guest unit @ 65%)	130
Tables Required (10 people per table)	20

SAMPLE BUDGET

ESTIMATED EXPENSES				
ITEM	**PER UNIT**	**UNIT**	**AMT**	**TOTAL**
Meal (inc tax & tip)	$58.71	person	200	$11,742
Entertainment	$500.00			$500
Postage	$0.49	env/2 mailings	800	$392
Printing / copying	$200.00			$200
Name Tags	$1.75	Person	200	$350
Centerpieces	$25	Table	20	$500
Decorations	$400			$400
Posters / Signs	$10		15	$150
Programs/Memory Book	$5	family	130	$650
Door prizes / Awards	$5	person	10	$50
A/V Equipment	$300			$300
Banner	$85			$85
Souvenirs	$1.00	person	200	$200
Insurance	$100			$100
Contingency (5%)	$100			$100
TOTAL EXPENSES				**$15,719**

ESTIMATED REVENUES				
ITEM	**PER UNIT**	**UNIT**	**AMT.**	**TOTAL**
Ticket sales	$85	person	200	$17,000
Item sales	$15	item	10	$150
Advertising	$20	ad	10	$200
Donations	$200			$200
TOTAL REVENUES				**$17,550**
REVENUES MINUS EXPENSES (Profit)				**$1,281**
COST PER PERSON				**$79**

(Cost per person represents expenses divided by estimated attendance and rounded up.)

Tables Required

Divide the expected turnout by 10. This is a standard number of seats per table. Check with the venue for what is recommended for their room layout. This will be necessary in determining how many centerpieces and table linens will be required.

Expenses

Room Rental, Meal Costs and Entertainment

If selecting a hotel or restaurant, the dance floor, tables and chairs, utensils, table linens, waiters and bartenders (above a minimum in bar sales) are included in the total per-person cost. However, if the facility requires renting these items, add these costs to the expenses.

Once the place and the menu are chosen, this will be the most important and largest reunion expense. (Be sure to include tax and tip in the total cost per person.) The cost of entertainment can be calculated by surveying professional disc jockeys (DJs). In our example, $500 was used as an average cost for hiring a DJ for four hours.

Printing, Copying, and Postage

Printing and copying costs, including stationery, envelopes, name tags, programs, and tickets, can be configured by estimating the number of mailings and the expected turnout. First class postage in the sample budget was based on a class size of 500, with two mailings.

- A 500-piece mailing to the entire group
- A 300-piece second mailing. This reduced amount assumes that a third of the envelopes in the first mailer will be returned with incorrect or unforwardable addresses

Photo Album or Memory Book
The cost of these items will be based on who is doing the most work.   For example, if a professional reunion photographer is hired who will also produce a photo book of the reunion, the cost could run anywhere from $8 to $30 depending whether it's done in black and white or in color.   A lot can be saved on a memory album or photo book if volunteers put forth most of the effort, leaving only printing costs.   Call reunion photographers for quotes.   Keep in mind, the committee has work to do as well. After the reunion, once the company producing the photo book sends the proofs, the committee oftentimes procrastinates on doing their part. See Chapter 15, *Wrap Up,* for ideas on creating a photo book or memory album.

Table Centerpieces
For live floral arrangements, call any florist for their price list. Helium balloons are popular and festive.   There are many balloon companies that cater large events and have designers who can suggest arrangements based on your budget.   Party stores also sell balloons and rent helium tanks.   Once final selections are made, the true costs for these items can replace the estimated ones.   The budget can then be reevaluated and, if necessary, adjusted.   If a tight budget is a factor, perhaps committee members can create centerpieces. This could be a fun project at a reunion meeting.

Decorations
Other decorations, such as a banner, posters, photo displays, etc., can be calculated by calling stationery stores and graphic design studios.   To save on this cost, perhaps creative committee members would make decorations.

Miscellaneous and Contingency
T-shirts, door prizes, name tags, audio/visual equipment, programs, thank you gifts, insurance, parking fees, and other miscellaneous costs should be included in the preliminary budget.

If anything is donated like door prizes, printing costs, stationery supplies, or auction items, these estimated expenses can be reduced or eliminated in the final budget. A category for all the little extras is judged at 2-3 percent of the total budget. Such costs might include bank account fees, office supplies, parking costs, committee meeting snacks, and meal and entertainment tips.

Total Expenses

In the sample budget, total expenses are estimated at $15,719 or about $79 per person.

Revenues

The ticket price must cover all estimated expenses. Remember to consider a price that most people would consider affordable. In our example, we chose $85 per person anticipating that this was both the maximum we could charge and the minimum we needed to include the features we envisioned.

Total Revenues

The figure for total revenues will be based mainly on ticket receipts. Think of proceeds from other sales such as t-shirts and photo books as icing on the cake. There will be additional income from higher ticket prices for latecomers paying at the door. However, it is recommended to use an average of the ticket prices when estimating revenues from ticket sales.

Advertising income from business card sales @ $20 per ad could generate $200 if 10 people respond. Sales from reunion items are trickier to estimate as the number of sales are unpredictable.

Ticket Price

Costs can be adjusted or eliminated; however, you must remember that once a ticket price is selected, this will be a cap for determining revenues. If there is a surplus, more can be spent on other items, such as centerpieces, souvenirs, memory album, or a charitable donation.

Fundraising Ideas

Maintaining a positive ending balance is the ideal goal. However, as the reunion approaches and cash may be running short, don't despair as there are ways to raise additional funds. Several ideas area described in this chapter, but please don't ask for donations at the reunion! This is bad management and a negative approach. Further, attendees will likely be reluctant to contribute at this point having spent so much just to get to the reunion.

First, refer to Chapter 2, *Organize Effectively*, for early fundraising ideas. Then, look for expenses that can be reduced or eliminated. Finally, read below for more some simple ways to raise money on short notice.

Donations

Request donations for those who can't afford to attend the reunion. Oftentimes, group members are pleased to contribute to those needing financial assistance, or just want to help with the reunion expenses. Furthermore, invitees who can't attend the reunion may also want to help.

Ask for donations toward specific items or categories such as postage, centerpieces, decorations, door prizes or other items. Announce these sponsors in the printed program and mailings or thank them during the reunion. While some donors may want to be anonymous, others may appreciate being thanked in front of their peers.

Business Card Directory

Include a section in the photo book or memory album for business cards and charge a nominal amount such as $25 per card. A variation on the theme would be to create a business card directory as a handout at the reunion. Charge a small fee such as $5 per entry and list the names and contact information. If some people want to include a full business card, charge more. A more elaborate presentation would be to include a yearbook or family picture. Be sure to thank contributors and encourage patronage of their businesses.

Raffles
A relatively easy and inexpensive fall-back for last minute fundraising appeals is to hold a raffle.

- A class yearbook or family heirloom. Many alumni have lost their yearbooks and would pay big bucks to get one back, even without the original autographs. In fact, a reunion is the perfect place to update those autographs or get some that were missed the first time around. Many would consider it the ideal opportunity and some may even feel it has more value.

- Specialty bottles of wine. (Sample custom labels in Chapter 9)

- Donations from local businesses such as dinner for two at an enjoyable restaurant, theatrical tickets, museum membership, movie tickets, or gift certificates at any local store. Charge a modest amount such as $1 per raffle ticket. Ask someone who has a "sales personality" on your committee to sell the tickets at the check-in table. Select the winner during the program.

One alumnus was planning her 30-year high school reunion. She wrote us that her 10-year-old daughter wanted to help so she had her sell raffle tickets at the reception table. While it was her husband who handled the money, it was her daughter's charming personality that helped bring in about $200 in raffle ticket sales.

Many establishments make donations to nonprofit organizations. While you don't have to file for nonprofit status, community businesses might be supportive of your reunion. Simply make a few phone calls and offer free advertising in the memory album, mailings, or reunion newsletter.

Reunion Items for Sale
Charge a few dollars extra for items being sold at the reunion, such as t-shirts, videos, cookbooks, photo albums, etc. If a vendor is handling sales, ask a friend or family member to help with cataloging the purchases.

If working with professional planners and needing additional funds to cover costs that are not included in the "packaged deal," work out a plan where they charge a few dollars extra per ticket and they reimburse the committee the overage.

Chapter 10 has more fundraising ideas for family reunions and Chapter 11 for military reunions.

The Reunion Planner Software Budget Report

If you have *The Reunion Planner®* software, input assumptions for all revenues and expenses. Then try different budget scenarios. After entering estimated expenses, adjust costs or the ticket price until a positive ending balance is achieved. With this budget report, you can reconcile the monthly bank statement. As actual expense dollars become known, this information can be entered into the estimated budget. Slowly, a more accurate appraisal of the financial situation will develop.

Balance Bank Statement with Actual Budget
    ✓   Reconcile the monthly bank statements

Nine Months before the Reunion

25%

6. Build a Foundation

Make the most out of committee meetings by being prepared beforehand. The chairperson should assess each individual's abilities and willingness to perform. Before each gathering, send out a reminder notice with an agenda of what needs to be accomplished. Include an estimated time frame. (See sample meeting notice in Chapter 2.)

Delegate tasks based on goals to be met. Afterwards, share a meal at a restaurant or someone's home. It's a nice thank you to volunteers since many arrange their schedules to be there. It is also a way to recap the success of your accomplishments.

Get the Word Out

Letting everyone know as soon as possible that a reunion is in the works will greatly increase the attendance potential.

Word of mouth is extremely important in promoting a reunion. With the variety of social media outlets, getting the word out about the reunion is simple, quick, and free. Certainly, for the social networking generation, these are the most widely used vehicles. Start a Facebook group page just for the reunion. Members will hopefully start the ball rolling. **Twitter** and **LinkedIn** are also good for generating buzz on the reunion. While it takes time and money, sending invitations in the mail is still an effective way to announce the reunion because it is more direct and personal.

To maximize attendance and outreach, we recommend using all possible vehicles to reach as many of your group's members as possible.

Add any details, pictures, and general reunion conversation on your dedicated Facebook page, post 'tweets' on **Twitter** with fun facts, and send emails with a link to the reunion website. All these broadcasts should generate excitement and greater interest in the event. If technically challenged in this area, ask a friend or family member to help.

U.S Postal Mailings

Over the past three months as addresses are being updated, the master list should be more current. If envelopes need to be hand addressed, as opposed to any number of software applications which print out labels in a jiffy, ask volunteers to address the envelopes prior to the meeting. If using labels, purchase a box of no less than 100 sheets. Avery labels and other brands are sold in a variety of sizes per page.

Send the first announcement to everyone. Use whatever addresses are known. For high school reunions, you will find that many parents still have the same address and can pass along reunion information to their children.

Include the statement **"Change Service Requested"** somewhere on the outside of the envelope. If mailing bulk rate, the fee for return service with a new address or reason for non-delivery is the current first class stamp. If mail sent with first class postage is received within a forwarding time frame, letters will be returned to the sender with the corrected address.

Several benefits can be achieved from this early mailing:
- Reservations with some early needed cash
- Personal histories for a memory album
- Pictures for the family history album, video, or display
- Addresses of yet more potential attendees
- Early word-of-mouth
- Additional volunteers to help with planning
- Early, discounted airline fares or group rate hotel arrangements

The First Mailing
The Announcement
Design the invitation. If using a computer, experiment with different fonts and graphics. If possible, use historic photos, related logos, mascots, or other identifying images for maximum nostalgic effect. If the reunion particulars are known at this time, define them.

Create First Reunion Announcement
    ✓   Create the reunion announcement
    ✓   Prepare a questionnaire or survey

Design the Invitation
- Date, place, length, and approximate starting time

- Cost per person or payment request

- This is a good opportunity to generate early revenues. Once a budget has been created, coming up with a ticket price will be easier. If known, include the following information:

  - o All the reunion particulars, schedule of events with dates and times, reunion location, and overnight accommodations,

  - o Ticket price (to encourage early reservations, designate cutoff dates for lower priced tickets.) Indicate how **checks should be addressed.**

  - o Reservation form

  - o Contact information for questions

Ask for donations to assist those in your group who may need financial assistance to attend the reunion, sponsor a charity or other non-profit, or make a contribution to the school alumni association.
- Payment acknowledgment. "If tickets are being paid online, a confirmation email will be generated. Otherwise, your canceled check is a receipt," or, "Tickets will be held at the door," or, "Tickets will be mailed about two weeks prior to the reunion."

- A deadline for any reservation refunds
- Any recommended attire
- Missing persons list

Optional or as needed:
- Questionnaire
- Reunion items for sale with price list
- Nostalgic pictures, memorabilia, or other items for display

Personal Data
- Last, maiden, first names, nickname (or name used when we knew you)
- Spouse or guest's name
- Number of guests in party
- Address, city, state, zip
- Email address
- Home, cell, and business phone numbers
- Location and/or contact of someone who will always know your whereabouts

Personal History for Awards, Questionnaire, or Survey
- If married, how long
- Children's names and ages
- Occupation
- Number of children, grandchildren, expecting date
- Distance of travel to the reunion
- Marry your high school sweetheart
- Proximity to the school, military base, or family homestead

Possible Memory Book Material
- Favorite teachers or commanders
- Pictures or photos from yesteryear
- Favorite song or musical group of the era
- Hobbies
- Funniest or most memorable lifetime event
- Anecdotes or stories from the olden days

One high school reunion committee included this question: "In high school I wanted to have a career as a _____. I ended up a _____." The most interesting responses can be included in the memory album.

If incorporating personal biographies into a memory or family history book, assign someone the task of editing and organizing the responses. Leave space on the questionnaire or on the reverse of the response sheet. Ask respondents to briefly describe what has transpired in their lives since you last met.

One high school reunion committee compiled a list of public issue-oriented questions and published the results in their memory album. Responses were entered into a database. The results were categorized and shown in percentages of the total class and by male and female responses. Occupations, education levels and views on topical issues were presented. It was a fascinating look at how perspectives had changed over time.

Questions Requiring Committee Follow-up
- Can you donate a door prize?
- Is there someone in the group who you know would like to attend the reunion, but cannot afford it? Assure respondents that answers will be kept confidential.
- Can you help on the reunion committee? List what is needed, e.g.. graphics, mailing, phoning, video montage assistance, set up, clean up, or online assistance.

Other Requests
- *Whom would you most like to see at the reunion?* Use the responses constructively. In other words, during the phone drive callers could say, "Dave Jones said he is hoping to see you at the reunion."
- *What teachers or officers would you like to invite to the reunion?*

- *What were your favorite activities?* Code common groups – the tennis team, drama club, chess club, swim team, etc. Add this information to the lists of members and note who will be attending the reunion under the headings of these groups.
- *Send in a current family picture for a photo collage.*
- *Can you provide any memorabilia, photos, recipes, quilting assistance, or slides for display at the reunion (or for use in family history documentation)? Ask respondents to clearly identify their property if they want it returned.*

Other Enclosures
- Response Label or Envelope. Make it as easy for guests to respond by providing a pre-addressed return envelope or label. To keep postage costs down, make sure this insert does not cause the mailing to weigh more than one ounce.
- Hotel or restaurant brochure
- Discount fares and other travel information

The First Mailing: What is Needed
Five or six people will be all that is needed to affix labels, fold, stuff, stamp, and seal the envelopes. The following items should be ready for the mailing meeting:

- **The Announcement with Inserts**
- **Envelopes**
  The mailing envelope (#10 size) should have a reunion identified return address labels affixed or printed on the upper left-hand corner. The recipient may be more likely to open or forward a reunion notification rather than treating it as junk mail if the sender is not easily recognizable. **Keep any returned letters for bad addresses.** Invalid addresses need to be logged in and followed up on, and the contents can be reused.

Select Best Mailing Address
✓ Under "Alumni Information Screen, For Labels Use." The "Main Address" is in fact the default address. Check "Alt Contact Address" if an alternate address is needed.

- **Return Envelopes**
  If it keeps the mailing under an ounce, include a pre-addressed return envelope (#9 size).
- **Address Labels**
  For the guest list and reply envelopes
- **Postage**
  Self-adhesive, first class stamps are preferable to bulk rate. First class mail arrives quicker, is forwarded and will be returned with a corrected address, if available. The letter will appear more personal and is less likely to be thrown away. A bulk rate permit requires cash up front, tedious sorting and weighing time and is much slower to arrive. Considering the cost and effort, is it worth the postage savings?

Print Mailing Labels
✓ Print out mailing labels and return labels

Entertainment
Musical entertainment at reunions is typical. It sets a festive mood for guests to mingle and socialize. Whatever entertainment is selected, book it as soon as the reunion date is locked in. This is especially important for summer reunions because many entertainers have engagements months in advance. We highly recommend not leaving this component to the last minute!

In selecting entertainment, consider the desired reunion ambiance. For instance, if reminiscing is the focus, is it necessary to offer dancing? Is an entertainer needed to act as a Master of Ceremonies, or will that job be offered to an alum or family member? If the purpose of the reunion is for everyone to get to know each other better, suggest guests bring musical instruments and plan a variety show with sing-alongs. Here are some ideas for entertainment:

Disk Jockey (DJ)
Depending upon how much the budget allows and the involvement level desired, a DJ can also act as a "Master of Ceremonies." Is it going to be necessary to have someone "warm up" the audience? Perhaps background music is all that's wanted. The cost can go from $500 and up, depending upon the number of DJs and the quality of the sound equipment.

Each DJ has his or her own style and a varied collection of music. Communicate clearly what is suitable for your group. Some DJs may have large collections of current songs but few from your era. Ask to see their song list to be sure your era is well covered. The DJ's age may be a good indicator of his predominant repertoire of songs. This is an important detail that can easily get overlooked. Some DJs "take over" an event. Is that what you want for your reunion? **Before hiring anyone, see them perform.**

Live Band
Again, the best indicator is to watch the musicians in action. Can they play songs from your era? In fact, inquire if they have entertained at reunions before. Do they intend to play recorded music during their break time? Some reunion committees choose to bring in their own music for filler during performance breaks.

Special appearances by entertainers that would be uniquely appealing to your group could spice up the event. Use whatever contacts committee members might have.

- An affordable musical group that was popular during your era and is still performing

- A popular radio DJ. Check the internet for reunion entertainers or call local public relations agencies and radio stations to see if any DJs are available for public appearances. Radio personalities make great MCs.

Jukebox
This can be different and a lot of fun, especially if children or guests representing a range of ages are attending.

Rent jukeboxes stocked with songs from any era or type designated. The music is nonstop and cheaper than live entertainment. This way, guests can select their favorite tunes during the event.

Computer-Based Continuous Music
Ask someone on the committee or in your group who is savvy or so inclined to acquire any favored songs and musicians of your era onto their laptop. The computer can be programmed to play your chosen songs continuously during the course of the event. Be sure appropriate speakers are available so the sound can be "amped up" for dancing, if need be.

For more ideas or referrals on entertainers, ask other reunion committees, catering managers of hotels, or friends who have hired similar entertainers.

Get referrals from other reunion committees or venues or check related websites for entertainers, orchestras, or bands. Whatever musical entertainment is preferred, be sure to get references. Better yet, go see them in action!

Once the entertainment is lined up, be sure they have the song preferences well before the reunion and double check the play list with them. Remind the sound person to keep the volume **LOW**. A common complaint at reunions is that background music is much too loud to hold conversations comfortably in the same room. Since reminiscing is the primary purpose of reunions, loud music can ruin the entire event.

Events, Activities, and Games

Below are some suggestions for reunion activities for class reunions. (Additional activities and games specific to family reunions are in Chapter 10 and Chapter 11 for military reunions.)

- Name tags were randomly handed out to arriving guests. During the evening, ask them to find the person belonging to the name tag.

- Introduce the sports teams and class officers. Ask them to lead everyone in singing the school song.

- Ask former football players and cheerleaders to lead everyone in school cheers.

- Bring elementary and middle school pictures from the feeder schools. Enlarge them on posters. Attendees from the same schools can reconnect and pose for group pictures.

- Provide activities or displays so spouses and guests or alumni can participate

- Hold a dance contest that doesn't require partners. This is an excellent ice breaker to get the dancing started.

- Show videos or DVDs from prior reunions. Let it play continuously during the evening.

- Invite teachers, coaches, or any special guests to say a few words during the program announcements

Video the Reunion Event

Many experienced videographers specialize in taping reunions. A reunion video would likely consist of a 90 minute to two hour video of candid shots of reunion activities, guest interviews, performances, and any program speeches, intertwined with era-specific background music. Perhaps they can insert old photos with then and now shots. Video companies often require a guarantee of sales and if that isn't met, be prepared to pay the minimum quota.

Videos usually sell well at reunions; however, to be certain, ask people in early reunion mailings if they would be interested in purchasing one. Costs can vary, so find a company that specializes in reunions and will travel.

If someone on the committee is knowledgeable and so inclined, he or she could create a video. Begin with a tour of the original stomping grounds. Continue with interviews of family elders, former teachers and coaches, or former armed services personnel. Include footage of activities and highlights from the yearbook or family photo album or from the last reunion. Show it at the reunion or finish it off with events from the current reunion. Post it on your reunion website, **YouTube**, or Facebook. Another option is to duplicate it on a DVD and take orders at the reunion. Otherwise, consider budgeting for an outside vendor so all reunion participants can relax and enjoy the event.

Video Montage

Another favorite at reunions is a pre-prepared video montage of historical and current pictures and activities. Hopefully, someone on your committee can put it together. Run it continuously throughout the event on one or more computer monitors to be viewed as the night progresses. It can be a lively point of conversation watching moments and people in their younger days.

Use pictures from the school yearbook, family album, or other historical perspective. Display it on a large screen either at dinner or during the program. Some locations may have screens.

Yearbooks
Bring yearbooks or other photo collections to the reunion. Some may have lost their yearbooks and will relish seeing them again. For those who missed the chance to sign any yearbooks, the reunion is the perfect opportunity to make that happen.

Photography
Some companies specialize in reunion photography and provide a photo booklet after the reunion. In choosing a photographer, ask to see a sample of their work. It should contain individual or couple portraits, candid shots for collage pages, along with a guest directory. Two photographers will reduce the waiting time.

Ask the photographer, family member, or other volunteer to also take candid shots for the collage pages because a professional photographer may miss some opportunities, and it is important to make sure everyone is included in the photo book. The book can be included in the ticket price or priced separately.

If someone in your group is, or knows, a professional printer, perhaps costs could be saved. Otherwise, selling ads from guests or local supportive enterprises could help defray the book's cost.

Since everyone has cameras and video recorders on their cell phones, and a booklet would be too expensive to produce, suggest guests upload their pictures to the reunion website, **http://shutterfly.com/photo-books**, Facebook, or other online media outlet.

Additional Casual Events
A casual event occurring before, on the day of, or after a formal evening event is an opportunity for smaller and more intimate gatherings and entire families to participate. It also gives those

who can't afford the gala event or have scheduling conflicts a chance to attend another reunion function. This gives people more time to reminisce or to catch up with those who were missed at another occasion.

A picnic in a park close to the main event would be ideal. School reunions could even have a picnic directly on the school grounds. We can't stress enough the importance of reserving a site early, as picnic areas or other venues may not be available. If outdoor activities such as a baseball game, Frisbee, soccer, or other group activity is planned, request that guests bring the applicable equipment.

When the details are known, mention the time and directions to the location of all events in any correspondence. Repeat the particulars in the reunion program, handouts, written itineraries, and on a sign at check-in.

Media Announcements
Begin placing announcements a year before the reunion. Post notices on websites of your school, alumni association, and focused online media that posts upcoming reunions. There are reunion websites that don't charge fees to do this.

Use the free reunion portal available on our website, **http://reunionplanner.com**, to announce your reunion to your group by sending email announcements linking to your webpage. This webpage should contain all the event information. In addition, include any photos or videos, blog posts, and blogging about your reunion as well as the option to purchase tickets. Include a "missing persons" list in case other guests using this page may know the whereabouts of anyone listed. It also allows for connections to Facebook, Twitter, and other social media.

Set up a webpage or create a Facebook group page. Be sure to keep this page private to your group. It can be as simple as posting the reunion details and adding pictures. Keep in mind not everyone will have a Facebook page, and frankly anyone above a certain age may not be as proficient or comfortable using such domains. Use whatever methods are easy and convenient to spread the word about the reunion while maintaining the privacy and security of your guests' information.

If working with professional planners, all payments and related reunion information will likely be available on their website.

Bank Account

The simplest most efficient way to handle reunion finances is creating your reunion website on **http://reunionplanner.com**, where ticket and item purchases can be paid via PayPal or credit card.

If your committee will be taking payments, open a bank account and set it up for online usage to pay bills, track the balance, and reconcile.

As an extra precaution, include the names of one or two committee members on the account with only one signature required to sign checks. Bookkeeping responsibilities include making copies of checks, depositing them, and recording all deposits and payments.

Organize the Paperwork

Even in this software age with everything available online or backed up in the "clouds," there usually is an accumulation of paperwork. It is good practice to organize any hard copies so information can be found easily and quickly by just labeling file folders and classifying any documentation. Folders might include the following:

- Committee rosters
- Printed master mailing list and phone list
- Contracts with vendors
- Personal biographies

- Copies of checks
- Bank statements
- Expense receipts
- Questionnaires and other responses
- Sale items
- Name tags
- Business cards
- Donators
- Copies of reunion announcements and media ads.

Update any changed or new information into the reunion Data section of the software.

Update any New Personal Information and Data
- ✓ Make name and address corrections
- ✓ Note any important comments
- ✓ Enter purchases and income
- ✓ Run budget software to check balances

7. Create an Ambiance

How do you stage an inviting event? The possibilities are endless. Since attending reunions can be costly for some, the justification for going must be strong enough to overcome any kind of objection. A higher turnout derived from creating an exciting ambiance will be based on the planners' ability to communicate and sell the event. Fresh new ideas will help convince potential attendees that the reunion is an event not to be missed. By adding a unique theme or inviting special guests, for example, you just might change those nay-sayers into yea-sayers.

Encompass a Theme
Since reunions are usually tied to a nostalgic event with historical significance such as a graduation, an elder family member's birthday, or military honor, a theme could be easily defined. Establish the reason for the reunion by applying an associated logo or idea to the invitations (see sample invitations in Appendix), decorations, souvenirs, and awards. Pictures of the school mascot, an ancestor's immigration record, or military insignia are some basic designs.

People are most likely to attend high school reunions in decades. Attendance at interim five-year reunions is typically the lowest. So, if a 15, 25 or 35-year class reunion is being planned, an enticing theme may be the incentive to come to the reunion.

Combine the Reunion with a Holiday

Depending upon the time of year the reunion is being held, you could accentuate a related holiday or season. For example:

- An elegant affair on New Year's Eve
- Valentine's Day motif in February
- Mardi Gras in March or April
- Western Hoedown with hayrides in May
- Fourth of July BBQ or picnic
- Costume party in October
- Thanksgiving weekend is a good excuse for any reunion
- Winter holiday theme in December

Social Action Project

A social action project is an excellent way to give something back to the community and to add purposefulness to your reunion. Suggest guests make contributions toward a particular foundation, charity, non-profit, a former school, scholarships, specific endowment, or other aid organization in honor of your group.

Family Project

A reunion that extends over several days will present a challenge in planning interesting activities. A theme day with related activities that any age can enjoy will work wonders. For family reunions, that could be a family tree project where everyone can participate. Suggest that everyone bring pictures and mementos. Hire a videographer or oral history expert to interview all attending family members, including children. Elder family members can tell stories and children can talk about their interests and interactions with grandparents in preparation of a family chronicle.

Honor Special Guests
The attendance of well-liked teachers or coaches may induce alumni to come to a class reunion. Invite a genealogist to speak at a family reunion. There may be a former admired officer that would enjoy chatting with past recruits and finding out about their current lives at military reunions. If any members of the group are accomplished in a particular field or association, or one of the guests had an illustrious career, highlight that entity or those people at the reunion.

If you've hired a well-known DJ, or invited an artist, speaker, genealogist, or other honored guest, include images from their website or Facebook page on your reunion announcements and flyers.

Mementos and Souvenirs
Reunions are opportunities to document personal histories and stories. There are a popular few formats. A memory album, video, genealogy chart, oral history, cookbook, quilt, and photo books are wonderful mementos and might even present the incentive to attend. Chapter 10 discusses mementos and souvenirs specifically designed for family reunions and Chapter 11 covers ideas specifically suited for military reunions.

Memory Album
Besides current and nostalgic pictures, a memory album can be a composite of life stories, poems, letters or essays, survey results, and a memorial page. This will be a cherished souvenir to hand out at the reunion. Depending on the cost to produce the book, it can be part of the ticket price or sold separately.

The simplest package is one that can be combined with a photo book prepared by the reunion photographer. Some photography companies specialize in reunions and offer packages to photograph the reunion and produce photo books of the event. Their standard book usually consists of a cover page, a committee picture with comments, couple and/or individual alumni pictures, three or four collage pages plus a directory or roster.

For a little more per book, add pages with you own design, such as: a memorial page, interesting anecdotes, nostalgic data like national events, fads, famous people, movies, books, songs, or a sampling of consumer prices back when. Then sell advertising space as a way to raise additional funds. Reprint business cards at a small fee per card.

For class reunions:
- Autobiographies collected in mailings next to each alumnus' yearbook picture
- Design a cover, a title page, and an introductory page. Include a mascot or other image as an identifying feature
- Add the reunion date and location on the title page
- The introductory page can have a welcome statement from the committee along with a group photo.
- Bring in collage pages of photos taken at the reunion
- Responses from the questionnaire, popular teachers, favorite songs, or other highlights from the era
- Incorporate yearbook or other related photos
- A memorial page of classmates who have passed on
- Any survey results
- Business card ads, list of contributors, or other acknowledgments
- Comments and feedback received after the reunion. Some samples are below.

> *"I loved how everyone hugged each other, even people who really never knew each other. We made several donations to local affiliations like the elementary school, a senior citizen center, the food bank, and the high school. It felt good to give back to the community in these little ways."*
>
> *"It was so much fun. I hugged more people in two days than I had in 20 years! I have never felt such a sense of love and belonging as I did at that reunion."*
>
> *"What a great event. After 30 years, we had no more pretenses; we just came to be together."*
>
> *"It was terrific. I reconnected with many old friends I was close to growing up and had known since elementary school."*
>
> *"The museum was a great venue. It wasn't a stuffy ballroom. I was afraid I wouldn't know anyone, but I got to see many of the guys I hung out with who were on the swim team and who I grew up with."*
>
> *"I'm just so glad I came. I really appreciated all the efforts so many made to get to the reunion."*

Once the design and content is complete, compare prices. Choose a printer with the best package. With the availability of desk top publishing software, the savings may be worth doing it yourself.

Name Tags and Buttons

Name tags are essential at reunions. Make as many tags in advance as possible. Yearbook pictures should be included for class reunions. Pictures make it easier to identify people; they stimulate introductions and conversations and serve as payment confirmation.

Button name tags are sturdy, nostalgic, and great souvenirs. Burton's Buttons, which you can find through our website at **http://reunionplanner.com/reunion-buttons**, offers custom-designed buttons, stickers, and lanyards along with personal attention and service. Otherwise, there are many websites that have such capabilities. Compare prices and check their reviews.

Name tags should not be smaller than three inches round or in length. Of the four offerings shown below, every guest gets a button at the reunion. Substitute the school mascot for those without a photo in the yearbook. Have several blank buttons on hand (with reunion information) for unanticipated arrivals. Use a Sharpie pen to inscribe names on buttons at the check-in table for any last minute arrivals.

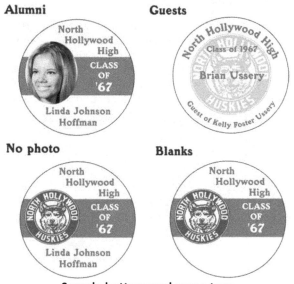

Sample buttons and name tags

Create Your Own
Photocopy yearbook pictures in high resolution. Alternatively, a copy shop can reprint photos on their superior machines. For greater visibility, enlarge the yearbook photos and lettering. (This is especially helpful for 25-year and up reunions.)

Print out guest's names that have been entered into a software program. Apply glue stick or rubber cement and affix or laminate the pictures on name tags. Place the tags in plastic badge holders sold in most stationery or office supply stores. These holders can be pinned or clipped onto clothing. Self-adhesive tags, Velcro strips, double sided tape, or other adhesive will generally only last for one wearing, if that.

It is recommended that military reunions include the division logo along with the ship or unit number. Family reunion name tags can have a family crest or be color coded to each family unit for easy identification.

Add Photos to Name Tags
    ✓ Import head shot photos into program to include on name tags.

Whatever approach is used, it is recommended that name tags be prepared in advance. Bring supplies to the reunion to make name tags for last minute arrivals.

In the interest of saving space, include only the maiden surname on the women's tags. If maiden and married surnames are preferred, accentuate the name most people will remember. Prepare name tags without pictures for non-members and spouses or for last minute walk-ins. Use letters large enough to be seen at a distance.

Tickets and Payment Acknowledgments

Physical tickets are not generally used for reunion admittance because they are an added cost to produce and mail. With online registration, email confirmations suffice. Workers at the registration desk should have a reservation list handy in case some guests missed a cut-off time or forgot their receipts.

On the other hand, physical tickets can be a nice memento. Tickets can easily be created on personal computers. Simply add a logo, family emblem, or other related photo. Tickets printed in color will make nice souvenirs. If you don't have a color copier, the result will be worth the cost of printing them at a local print shop.

A less expensive method would be to use a roll of movie ticket stubs to be given to each guest in their registration packets. These are available at most party or stationery stores. The double rolls are best for door prize ticket stubs.

If tickets are not sent out in advance, indicate how admittance will be handled in any reunion correspondence. For example, "Your canceled check is your receipt," or, "Your tickets will be held at the door." Many event coordinators use the registration packets as "tickets" and the name tags act as proof of payment for the meal. A reservation or attendance list at the check-in table should serve as another verification of payment.

If physical tickets are not used, some acknowledgement of payment should be conveyed. A quick email should be sufficient. If credit cards are accepted on a website, the software will probably email a receipt to the purchaser and also to the reunion coordinator.

Accounting Guidelines

Record payments promptly. The bulk of the ticket money will usually arrive close to the deadline with the lowest ticket price and again just before the reunion as some people inevitably wait until the last minute to pay or even decide whether or not to attend. If guests mail in checks, make copies for the record in case a question comes up later.

Enter all Purchases, Confirm with an Email

- ✓ Enter all receipts for each person as payments arrive.
- ✓ Print address labels for paid guests if sending receipts or tickets for confirmation of payment
- ✓ Send Email confirmation

8. Encourage Attendance

The larger the attendance, the more exciting the reunion! Reunion memories are more highly cherished as the ratio of recognizable guests increase. A common goal among reunion enthusiasts is to get as many people as possible to attend the reunion. Careful investigation and perseverance will result in a high turnout. Ideas for finding people are in Chapter 4. This chapter focuses on encouraging those who have already been found to attend the reunion.

Use every means possible to encourage reunion attendance – attractive mailers, personal contact through phone drives, media announcements, social media notices, and word of mouth. We also offer responses for those who, initially, might be reluctant to attend; in other words, *"Don't take no for an answer."*

Make the Reunion Enticing
Making your reunion sound like the event not to be missed involves skillful communication. Inviting special guests and having appealing entertainment and fun activities are all strong selling points. While social media is efficient, simple, and free, direct mail will have a greater impact. It also helps to make the announcements graphically interesting as well as informational.

Broadcasting the Reunion
Encourage input by soliciting ideas on possible reunion locations or entertainment ideas. Send a questionnaire well before actual planning takes place. Good ideas will come of it, and more people will feel part of the event if they had a role in planning it.

Direct mail is the most prevalent method of informing people about a reunion. Make the notices eye catching, informational, and interesting. Include illustrations: a high school mascot or emblem, the family crest, or a military service logo. Use computer clip art. If a theme party like a "sock hop" is planned, embellish the invitations with related drawings or images.

The Phone Drive
Making personal contact with as many potential attendees as possible will boost the attendance immensely. It is easy to ignore or forget about written correspondence. A phone call from a familiar person is always more effective. This lets the person know how much their presence is desired. Much of that will be missing, however, if professional reunion planners do all the solicitation work. Remember, it takes effort if you want a quality reunion.

Try to organize one meeting per month for the phone drive. Holding monthly meetings at someone's office to make calls will accomplish a great deal. Camaraderie will bolster callers because people are always more focused and motivated working together on a common goal. Even if just two or three people can meet to make calls, the time will be well spent. Meeting regularly also helps to remind, nudge, and focus attention on the reunion. If meeting regularly is not feasible, divide the phone lists among committee members to make calls at home.

As the committee members are making calls, remind them to ask for any information on the whereabouts of the "missing." Getting a phone number for someone who will always know how to  reach them will also be helpful. Callers should note all responses from phone drives on their lists. These comments will be very useful for future phone drives. Ask callers to please be responsible for giving any "new" information (address, phone, or name changes) to the person in charge of updating the main address list.

Print Phone Lists for Committee Members to Call

   ✓ Print phone lists and divide it among all volunteers. The lists can be sequenced by area codes to control toll calls

   ✓ Write down responses and follow-up details in the comment section.

   ✓ Add contact information of someone who will always know your guest's whereabouts

Regular phone calls also help with some following roadblocks.

- **Procrastination and indecision.** People put things off until the last possible moment. In fact, even when people live close to where the reunion is being held (since they don't need to make travel arrangements), many still will not commit to going until the day before the reunion. Repeated reminder calls will help solve this problem and perhaps lessen last minute food ordering dilemmas which inevitably occur. Valerie Anderson from Salt Lake City, Utah lamented,

  "I definitely felt like I was in a catering nightmare when I heard through the grapevine that 50 more people were coming than had responded."

- **Forgetfulness or disorganization.** Many people misplace, lose, or put aside mail that doesn't require immediate attention. Again, a personal phone call is hard to ignore and people are generally happy to be reminded.

The Second Mailing

Update the mailing list with any new information before sending out the second announcement. While several responses may have been generated from the first announcement, this mailing will go to everyone even if it is just a reminder of the reunion minus those whose letters were returned.

The Announcement
If working with professional planners, be sure to insist that non-revenue generating event details are included in all notices. They may not be attentive to such events if their fees are not tied to ticket sales.

Payment Request
If ticket payments haven't already been requested, do so now. To encourage early responses, set one or two deadlines with discounted fees. A sample payment schedule might look like this for a June 10th reunion date:

> <u>Two price breaks</u>
>
> | | |
> |---|---|
> | By April 30th | $60 person, $110 couple |
> | By May 31st | $65 person, $125 couple |
> | At the Door | $70 person |
>
> <u>One price break:</u>
>
> | | |
> |---|---|
> | By May 1st | $60 person |
> | June 1st and thereafter | $70 person |

Protocol for Cancellations
Provide a deadline for cancellations and refunds. Closer to the reunion, it is usually difficult to return funds as the money will likely be tight. Of course, this can be discretionary depending upon the personal situation and the balance in the bank account.

List of Missing Persons
Print and include a list of those still needing to be found in all mailings. Post this list on the reunion website and update the list as soon as contact information has been verified.

Print List of Missing Persons
- ✓ Identify all alumni with known addresses as 'Found'
- ✓ Mark as 'Found' all those who responded
- ✓ Print list of 'Alumni Not Found'

Hotel Flyer or Information on Accommodations

If a discounted room rate is negotiated with the reunion venue, ask if the hotel has a small flyer for this notice. It should be lightweight enough to keep the mailing under an ounce. Otherwise, just include the overnight accommodation information and the group's discounted room rate in the announcement. Provide a link to the hotel website on the reunion webpage too.

Address Labels and Envelopes

As with the first mailing, a #10 envelope should serve as the main mailer. To avoid using envelopes, an 8 ½ x 11 inch newsletter or one page notice can be folded in thirds and stapled or taped. As was mentioned earlier, be sure to omit address labels for those whose first mailer was returned.

Print Mailing Labels for Second Mailing
- ✓ Print labels for all "Found" alumni
- ✓ Print address labels of the reunion headquarters for reply cards or envelopes

Return Envelopes

If there is room for inserts, include a return envelope; #9 size works best. Print return address labels or use the committee's return address rubber stamp.

Postage

In calculating the necessary postage, make sure to exclude the amount of returned letters from the first mailing.

How to Encourage Hesitant People to Attend

Undoubtedly, as reunion guests are contacted, it will happen that some people are reluctant to attend apart from any geographical, financial, or scheduling reasons. Bewildering disinterest is one problem all reunion organizers face. Committee members work hard to make the reunion special, so any indifference can be quite disheartening. Apprehensions can range from reunion ambivalence to reluctance at being seen. Such anxieties could stem from high school insecurities, fears that they might not be as successful as desired, or alumni feel they don't look as good as they would like.

Of course, there are the exceptions (some people never change) or the nay-sayers who fervently profess not ever to attend a high school reunion for any number of reasons. Unfortunately, it is a major loss for those who would like to see them and for themselves as they miss out on an infrequent life milestone.

Listed below are a few replies to some common concerns. Let the volunteer committee members be aware of some of the following excuses so they can be prepared with an appropriate response.

"I don't know if I'll remember anyone."

Reassure them that not only will they see former friends and classmates, extended family members, military buddies, etc., there will be people we forgot we knew. Also, assure them that names tags with yearbook pictures will be worn. Have the list of names of those attending or interested in attending handy while making calls, because during the phone drive, others may have expressed a desire to see them!

"I probably don't have anything in common with people I haven't seen in ___ years."

Fill in any number. The answer will be the same. It is amazing how much we **do** have in common with people we haven't seen in many years. Most of us have changed, and once you connect, you will truly enjoy seeing those who shared your formative years, even if it is only at a reunion.

"Nothing has changed in my life. I am too embarrassed to go."

Many are disheartened if they've had little progress in their lives. Let them know that people are going to great efforts to come to the reunion and traveling long distances hoping to see them! People don't see what we have or haven't accomplished, they just see the person they once knew.

"I'm too fat. I look old. I'm divorced and unhappy. I'm unemployed, etc."

The beauty of attending a high school reunion is that most of us are stunned to find out that all those fears and anxieties, sometimes still prevalent 10, 20, even 30 years later, were just that, teenage angst. But for many, we don't learn this until we actually attend a reunion and discover that most people just want to share stories and laugh with us about those crazy days.

The amazing thing is we all have the same fears and shortcomings. This is why reunions are so therapeutic to our lives. People discover that no one cares about how you look, your checkered past, or your employment status. They just want to see you. It's confidence building knowing people just care about seeing you no matter what your perceived imperfections.

> *"Some people didn't want to come because of the weight they had gained, so we started telling people we weren't charging by the pound. Everyone found that amusing and those who had concerns came anyway."* —Valerie Anderson

"I hated that time of my life, why should I go to a reunion and be reminded about it?"

The reunion is an excellent opportunity to dispel old fears and haunting memories. After seeing former classmates and rivals as adults who have the same problems and experiences, former jealousies and resentments not only fade, they disappear. In fact, this may be a healing process for many.

Letting go of old resentments and intimidations is not easy. Nevertheless, a reunion may be the perfect opportunity to allay such fears and begin the healing.

"No one I know will be there"

Another common reaction to avoiding a reunion is they think that no one they were close with will attend. Tell committee members to ask such skeptics who they would like to see at the reunion. If the whereabouts are known, encourage the ambivalent one to contact them. If their whereabouts are not known, get any additional information on the "missing one" so the sleuths on the committee can try to locate them. Also, someone may show up that they forgot they knew, and will undoubtedly be happy to reconnect with them.

The truth is that once hesitant people get to their reunions, they usually have a wonderful time. They just need to give themselves the opportunity.

The committee may have more ideas to encourage people to attend. Good luck, try not to get discouraged, and don't give up on anyone too easily.

Six Months before the Reunion

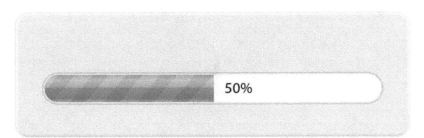

50%

9. Reunion Decor

As the event draws nearer, attending to details takes on greater urgency. Attention to the reunion decor is as important as the entertainment, and it doesn't cost as much. Choose a decor that reflects comfort and fun.

Decorations, Displays, and Mementos
Balloons
Balloons are the staple for reunion centerpieces. They are inexpensive and quite festive. Large individual clumps of balloons at the entryway and around the room give the impression of fun.

Table Centerpieces
Refer to the budget for the allotment of table centerpieces. Come up with design ideas that will fit. Perhaps someone in your group is artistic and can help.

Floral Arrangements
This could be costly on a limited reunion budget. However, a small arrangement of balloons and colorful metallic paper with a few fresh flowers can be put together shortly before the reunion and will be more affordable.

When working with professional planners and additional funds are needed to cover an expense that isn't in their "packaged deal," work out an arrangement where they charge a few dollars extra per ticket and reimburse the committee for the overage.

If the reunion is in May or June, order the flowers quite early because these months are the busiest in the floral industry with weddings and Mother's Day. In selecting a florist, look at pictures of other similar events they have handled. The hotel or restaurant sponsoring the reunion may have a list of florists they recommend.

Decorative Display of Class, Family, or Nostalgic Photos
It is festive and creative to include photos from the era or event being recognized. Arrange several photos, mementos, and other nostalgic artifacts in a decorative display. It should stimulate lively conversations related to the occasion and make good souvenirs.

Balloons alongside Centerpieces
Vendors can deliver or assemble the helium balloons on the day of the reunion. Check with the location for the soonest the room will be available that day. Since set up time on the day of the event will be valuable, we recommend leaving the chore of inflating balloons to the experts.

Wicker Baskets Filled with Colorful Paper
Anchor helium balloons to a heavy object inside a basket. Make copies of important documents related to your event: a graduation program, diploma, passports, the family matriarchs, pictures of commissioned posts, ships, etc. They could be laminated and attached to decorative stands. Scatter colorful confetti on the table.

Flowers, Potted Plants, Desserts, and Themed Display
Decorative pots filled with attractive plants could function as centerpieces, door prizes, or even an auction item. The door prize winner is the one with a sticker under his or her chair.

Sweets, candy, or cupcakes can serve a dual function as centerpieces and dessert.

Wine Bottles with Personalized Labels
A good bottle of wine with a personalized label can serve multiple functions. Add balloons, ribbons, and other accents. This unique display and/or door prize will be a hit at any reunion. A winery in California called **Windsor Vineyards** produces excellent bottled wines and will put any inscription, logo, or picture on the labels. However, they can only deliver to 42 states. Check for wineries that may handle all 50 states. Two samples follow:

Sample wine bottle labels provided by Windsor Vineyards.

Festive centerpiece

Banners

A vinyl or canvas banner is strong enough to last for many reunions. For under $100, you will have a permanent spirited welcome to arriving guests. Check online, with local sign companies, printers, or our website for custom banners. Paper signs are less expensive, but for long term usage, we recommend vinyl, canvas, or a cloth sign. It will be well worth the initial investment.

Another display could show the reunion statistics such as "who came the furthest" as part of the centerpiece on each table.

If planning a sit-down dinner, consider having a seating chart. While it involves more work, it is definitely a crowd pleaser. This way, everyone knows where people who showed up are sitting. Enlarge a picture of the seating chart and mount it on foam core for display on an easel near the check-in tables, or provide a list of attendees with their table numbers inside each registration envelope.

Posters

Poster sized copy of senior class group photo

For a nostalgic touch, use pictures from the yearbook, the family tree, or earlier family reunion group photo, military squadrons, naval ship crews, etc. Have them enlarged and mounted on poster boards. A class group photo (sample above) is always fun as everyone tries to find themselves. Smaller versions of the same photos, or others, such as an army base, passport photos, old newspaper stories, immigration papers, or other related materials, on 8 x 10 inch table tent centerpieces will contribute toward the ambiance. Check with the facility on their rules for using nails or tacks on the walls. Easels and bulletin boards may be the best alternative.

Display movie posters popular during the time of graduation or event being celebrated. A store in Hollywood, California, has a large selection of movie posters at costs ranging between $10 and $600, depending on their popularity. You can take a look their website, by going to **http://hollywoodbookandposter.com**, or call for availability and prices on posters from a specific era. Located on Hollywood Boulevard, they are appropriately called Hollywood Movie Posters, (323) 463-1792. **Allposters.com** also has an array of nostalgia movie posters for reasonable prices that would definitely liven up the room décor. For some real classics, visit **http://movieposter.com** for vintage movie posters before 1980.

Nostalgia Table

For any reunion, memories of times past are a central focus throughout the event. A table with various nostalgic artifacts is easy to set up. For class reunions, look for varsity athlete sweaters, yearbooks, school newspapers, uniforms, regulation booklets, the graduation program, letters from classmates unable to attend, photo albums from previous reunions, books, dedications, etc.

Hand-made quilts and nostalgic pictures at family reunions are especially poignant. Ask guests to send in photos for display and write their names on the back of their pictures to ensure that they are returned to the rightful owners.

Napkins, Linens, Glassware

Cocktail napkins and coasters in the appropriate colors imprinted with the school logo, family name, or other identifying feature with the date of the reunion is an inexpensive and pleasant memento. These items can be ordered at most print shops, party supply, or stationery stores.

If the facility provides table linens and napkins, select the preferred colors. If renting linens from an outside vendor, check the budget to verify that linen napkins are affordable. While linen is more elegant, colorful paper napkins will serve the same purpose.

Outside caterers can provide the dinnerware, glassware, and silverware. If an elegant route is preferred, add this expense in the per person food cost; otherwise, heavy-duty plastic ware will suffice. The caterer should provide drinking water, pitchers, glasses, and coffee cups. Again, if an elegant dinner presentation is not important, plastic plates, glasses, and cups still work. Just be sure to include the supplies in your budget.

In Memorandum

It is always a kind tribute to remember those in your group who have passed on. A display of their names and photos would be a respectful acknowledgment. Memorial posters at reunions are a reminder that life can be fleeting and we can appreciate our relationships and friendships, especially at reunions. Photos can be scanned and transferred onto a poster. Many print shops can produce such a remembrance with pictures from the yearbook. Simply pin it up on a wall or mount it on a poster board to display at the reunion.

Example memorial poster

Special Honors

Use the reunion to honor individual members of your group for their humanitarian accomplishments, community service, leadership experience, or military service. Whether it is classmates, family, or other members of your group, take a moment during the reunion to give them special recognition. At this class reunion, each attending veteran was presented with a personalized plaque thanking them for their service. (See high school yearbook picture poster of veteran classmates on the following page.)

It is never too late to appreciate our veterans. Indeed, it would be especially significant to recognize and thank them amongst their peers.

Solicit written memories from alumni whose lives were impacted in a positive way by specific teachers or administrators. Equally worthy is to honor any of your group's members for their community service, volunteer activities, or work in philanthropic endeavors. Highlighting or providing a focus at the reunion of special contributions or accomplishments by members of your group sets an example on the value of charity and selfless deeds to our children and future generations.

Poster honoring alumni veterans displayed at the reunion

Equipment Needs
Dance Floor and/or Section Dividers
A dance floor is usually basic at class reunions. It is a fun ending to an evening spent chatting it up with old friends. Most facilities with banquet halls have them. If not, rent one. Check a few rental agencies for prices. There may be an additional charge if an after hours pick up is necessary.

If the room doesn't provide a clear separation between the dining tables and reception area, consider renting section dividers or lattices. This will help the flow of the event and enhance the appeal of the dining area.

Audio Visual Equipment
Many restaurant or hotel facilities will rent audio visual equipment to groups holding events at their location. An outside vendor will most likely need to pick up their equipment that evening, which may incur additional costs. If AV equipment is needed, verify that the location has the electrical power and accessibility, especially if the reunion is outdoors.

Insurance

An event facility that is neither a hotel nor a restaurant will probably require event liability insurance. This is a good idea. It protects the committee sponsoring the reunion as well as the facility. Purchasing a one-day-event policy may cost a few hundred dollars, but shop around with insurance agencies. Adding a rider to a committee member's homeowner insurance policy might be another option. If someone has a good relationship with an insurance agent or broker, see if they can find an affordable plan.

Reunion Items for Sale

Offering items to sell can help raise additional funds. Besides offering mementos and helping to balance the bank account, having a financial cushion will help to:

- Cover miscellaneous or unforeseen expenses
- Give a donation to a charity, your alma mater school, or other organization supported by the group.
- Maintain a stipend for the next reunion.

All parties benefit. The committee gets additional cash and people go home with appreciated mementos. Specialty items to order in bulk might include a video of the reunion, coffee cups, t-shirts, sweatshirts, pens, baseball caps, etc. Items the committee could personally make and sell are family cookbooks, booklets with pictorial tributes, family tree charts or videos, quilts, or other customized hand made artifacts.

If the reunion date is inscribed on the item for sale, it must be sold during the current reunion. However, if the date and place are left off, the items can be sold at subsequent reunions.

Alternatively, if inscriptions are imprinted on glassware, for instance, the item can also be an award or door prize or even a gift to an especially hardworking committee member. In fact, the entire reunion committee should get a memento as an appreciation for all their work on the reunion.

T-shirts, Sweatshirts and Golf Shirts

T-shirts, sweatshirts, and/or golf shirts are perfect as reunion souvenirs because anybody can wear them and they're affordable and profitable. T-shirts can be ordered in preferred colors with logos, emblems, or photographs.

Design the t-shirt with the names of classmates inside the year of graduation.

Depending on the expected turnout, t-shirt vendors can bring pre-made t-shirts to the reunion. If they sell out of their supply, they can always order more. Another option is to purchase them for arrival by reunion time to sell at the reunion. Mention them in early mailings to estimate how many to order and what sizes.

The Reception Procedure

It is a distinct advantage to have enthusiastic volunteers greeting guests at the registration tables. Friendly greeters immediately put people at ease. It also creates an important "good first impression" especially for anyone who may be feeling a bit awkward or nervous. In fact, it probably sets the tone for the whole event.

Registration responsibilities include checking people in, handing out packets (and possibly souvenirs), collecting payments, and directing guests to the event.

Committee members can assume these roles; however, if they prefer not to, perhaps spouses, friends, co-workers, or family members can help. Someone from the committee should be near the area to deal with any questions or problems.

At one 25-year high school reunion, children of alumni were dressed in the school's lettermen sweaters and greeted people as they arrived. This provided a welcoming ambiance for arriving guests.

Try to enlist more people than you think is necessary to work at the registration tables. By reunion time, if it turns out fewer people are available, there should be enough coverage. Extra assistance will reduce errors and waiting time and allow workers to take breaks or work shorter shifts.

Depending on the expected turnout, it's probably best to have at least three to five people handing out registration materials. Attention should be directed to one person handling payments, especially if cash is involved. Such assistance will minimize errors and lessen the wait time.

Another idea for reducing the eventual logjam at check-in, as the bulk of attendees arrive, is to direct guests to posters or other displays that may answer questions that inevitably come up.

"Our check-in table always gets backed up because everyone wants to know who is there or if so-and-so has arrived yet. We directed anyone who asked, to the list of posted names we created of all guests who signed up. It also helped to have someone check off guest's names as they arrived."

Grammar school pictures blown up for poster displays

10. Family Reunion Basics

Planning a family event for people that don't see each other very often is probably close to the top of the personal stress meter. Family reunions, as opposed to class reunions, can entail many different emotions that have long-lasting effects. Being related to those you are reuniting can inspire great accolades or radically alter the family dynamics. How's that for pressure?

This chapter offers planning ideas tips based on the uniqueness of family reunions.

The Focus of a Family Reunion

Family reunions often take place over several days and are attended by diverse age groups. Activities, games, meals, and entertainment must suit a variety of tastes and personalities. Depending on the focus of the reunion, documenting or updating the family history is likely a priority.

List the family's requirements. Make organizational decisions based on those evaluations. For example, are these annual events or infrequent occasions? What is the objective or theme?

Family Reunion Objectives
- Bring members together for the first time
- Celebrate a special family occasion
- Document family history
- Study genealogy
- Celebrate a homecoming
- Honor a special achievement
- Form bonds that distances prevent
- Get to know each other better

Whether one or more reasons apply to your situation, some of the following concerns may need to be addressed:

- Where are most family members living?
- Are there financial constraints?
- What are reasonable travel costs for the group?
- What is the minimum person count to cover all costs?
- Are there supportive family members that can help plan different portions of the event?
- Are there any special considerations, i.e. disability or accessibility issues?
- Is there a wide diversity of ages?

Planning a family reunion also requires effective organizational skills. Refer to Chapter 2, Organize Effectively: *strategize, structure,* and *streamline.*

When and Where
As the expression goes, "Timing is everything." Is there a unique occasion being celebrated? For example, is this a special anniversary, birthday, combination of birthdays, a retirement, a return from living overseas, or other milestone event? Using a theme to plan a family reunion is a practical justification that offers an incentive to attend.

An event that coincides with another important family occurrence such as a wedding, confirmation, bar/bat mitzvah, christening, or graduation is a convenient reason to get people together and an opportune time to plan a reunion.

If the reunion does not involve a specific event, consider a time of year that allows for activities to occur both indoors and outdoors. However, be prepared for inclement weather. If people are forced to stay inside for long periods with nothing to do but talk, there should be plenty of indoor activities on hand. While reunions are meant for gathering and talking, long-term communal confinement could be counterproductive.

Four days is a suitable time frame if this is an infrequent or first time gathering of the family clan. However, an annual park or backyard barbeque can be just as memorable.

Family Reunion Locations
In choosing a location for a family reunion, consider a spot where the bulk of family members live or that has a special significance to the family. Consider characteristics like your hometown, where a contingent of ancestors lived, or perhaps an entry port where your predecessors immigrated.

If family is spread all over the country, select an affordable retreat to enable guests to focus their financial resources on travel. If feasible, visit the location, or at a minimum, get a recommendation from someone you know who has stayed there.

Chapter 3 contains ideas for reunion locations. Choose one that can easily adapt to groups and offers enough space where everyone is not forced to be together all the time. Small meeting areas for those wanting quiet moments will be sufficient. Having a supermarket nearby will also be helpful, along with interesting site-seeing locales for free time excursions.

The retreat should have 911 services, a nearby emergency room, name and number of a dentist available nights and weekends, hospital equipment supply if a wheelchair or crutches need to be rented, and the name, address, and phone number of the nearest 24-hour pharmacy.

A site that caters to family reunions will have an event coordinator to help with planning events, games, and activities. Check for minimum reservation room requirements.

Ethnic Reunions
Celebrate the Family Culture

Ever considered holding or attending an ethnic reunion? One way to acknowledge and appreciate the family history is to celebrate your family culture. Many family groups reunite to celebrate their heritage with folk dancing, ethnic foods, art, exhibits, music and sports traditions, and customs. Some also hold discussions on their cultural history, foods, genealogy, and language.

Ethnic reunions occur in the United States and overseas in different locations every year. One unique American landmark is Ellis Island, the major port of entry for 17 million immigrants between 1892 and 1954. A major part of America's history, this 27-acre island has a main building with over 4,000 exhibits and artifacts and a baggage room with original trunks and suitcases. The Great Hall tells the story of where 90 different nationalities waited for inspectors to review their entry documents and be examined by doctors.

Many families meet relatives at European cultural reunions that they never knew existed. Many such reunions take place every year throughout the United States. Finnfest reunions (celebrating the Finnish heritage) have occurred annually since 1983. Finns and Finnish Americans celebrate their heritage with music, folk dancing, entertainment, foods, gifts, and memorabilia. Their hope is to encourage descendants to recognize, appreciate, and continue their family tradition. Contact: FinnFest USA, **http://finnfestusa.org**.

Greek, German, Italian, Scottish, and Irish Fests, **http://irishfest.com**, regularly occur as well. They honor their unique traditions and customs by bringing people of similar cultures together, providing forums for genealogy research, and raising money to maintain their rich heritage for future generations. The upstate New York Italian Cultural Center and Museum, for example, grew out of a desire to tell the story of the Italian immigrant. This nonprofit organization is sponsored by the

American Italian Heritage Association and houses memorabilia, artifacts, and old photos for the US Italian American community, **http://americanitalianmuseum.org.**

The African American community is probably the oldest and largest ethnic group that holds regular organized family reunions. The African American Family Reunion Conferences celebrate principles, traditions, and family unity in their regular three-day conferences. They feature workshops, speakers, and resources in family reunion planning. This helps strengthen family bonds and community ties. For more information, contact Black Meetings & Tourism, 20840 Chase Street Winnetka, CA, 91306M. Phone: (818) 709-0646. Fax: (818) 709-4753. Website: **http://BlackMeetingsandTourism.com**

Enticing Announcements
Include an itinerary and description of the planned activities in all mailings. This will help generate interest and initiate responses. If physical invitations are being mailed out, design or choose one that is attention-grabbing and creative. There are many websites that have a variety of invitations specific to family reunions. Look for one that is relevant to your reunion theme.

Sample Family Reunion Invitation focusing on developing a family tree.

Besides providing the details on the reunion event, make the mailings newsy and engaging. Add any of the following:

- An itinerary and description of all planned activities
- A questionnaire
- The latest marriage, birth and death announcements
- Prior reunion photos
- Clip art, jokes, family oriented poems
- Children's art
- Stories and family trivia
- Suggested attire for various events
- Request donations for family members in financial need
- A directory of contact information for all members

Include a family photo from the last reunion and let everyone know what to wear for this year's group photo.

The reunion could also be an opportunity to create or update a family project that would be available at the event. In fact, if some family members are ambitious, it could also be an ongoing project that gets updated at each successive reunion. Such projects could be one or more of the following:

- Information and photos for the family history book or video recording
- Recipes for the family cookbook
- Individual, personalized quilt squares for the family quilt
- Family tree information for the genealogy chart

Registration
As discussed earlier, the initial reception sets the tone for the entire reunion. Greet arrivals with signs or banners. Whatever methods are used, make the initial greeting a welcomed and positive experience. Highlight the reason for reuniting on all registration handouts. Whether it's an anniversary, a birthday or just getting together, include something that reminds guests why they're there. It is highly recommended that everyone wear name tags, including greeters, all the time. Related or not, everyone needs assistance on remembering names, and it could prove embarrassing to err.

Set up a bulletin board in a central location with announcements of each day's activities and suggested times so everyone can plan their schedules accordingly. This could be the focal point of the reunion. Include a memorabilia table here with displays, artifacts, and pictures.

Name Tags
Name tags are important at any reunion. For a multiple-day reunion, they should be sturdy enough to be reattached each day. Button, laminated, or cloth name tags work the best.

Events, Games, and Activities
The main purpose of prearranged games and activities at family reunions is to provide a setting for people to talk. For multiple-day reunions, it will be challenging to plan activities that keep people interested and busy.

Start with an ice breaker. If family members brought their home videos and pictures, this might be a good opportunity for everyone to get to know each other better.

Meals

Sketch out several meals together, such as breakfast and dinner. Allow people to be on their own for lunch. Don't have every day filled with organized activities; people need to have time to enjoy some normal things they do while on vacation.

Based on how many people are attending the reunion, a fun activity would be to ask two or more immediate families to be responsible for a meal for the entire group. For example, assign specific family groups to choose the menu, shop, prepare, and cleanup for each breakfast, lunch, and dinner that is being shared. This will save time and money and help formulate closer bonds, especially for families who may not see each other that often or get to attend many reunions.

Bring the Children

Don't assume that children will develop their own games and activities during the reunion. Plan a few activities to allow family members of all ages to be together and some designed for children and adults to enjoy separately. Sharing common interests builds bonds and warm memories if children and teenagers can connect with each other on their own level.

Outdoor Activities

Ask everyone to bring their own sports equipment even if they are holding the reunion at a lodge or hotel that has these items. Depending on the location, ask guests to bring appropriate equipment. Tennis, basketball, bicycling, soccer, volleyball, badminton, tag, football, bocce ball, golf, Frisbee, croquet, or softball gear are some great ideas.

Of course, children can bring their own skateboards, roller blades, ice skates, fishing accessories, and other sports equipment.

Depending on the site's options, team sports might include basketball, softball, or soccer. Select a location with a swimming pool or near a lake or river for boating activities. The kids love to swim and everyone can enjoy the related activities. Be mindful that adults need to be in constant supervision of children who are involved with water activities.

Depending upon the time of year, activities can involve both children and adults. Scavenger or treasure hunts, croquet, golf, horseback riding, skiing, ping pong, archery, and shopping are a few activities everyone can enjoy. Egg or water balloon tosses, sack and relay races, softball, volleyball, and badminton are appropriate for all ages, even if some participants are just spectators.

Quick Tip: A suggestion for all age groups. Here's a race that doesn't force people to compete directly against each other and involves several skill levels. Select a fixed route upon which different modes of transportation can coexist like walkers, runners, bicyclists, and parents pushing baby strollers. Each group starts 10 minutes apart. Each person estimates their individual completion time. The winner is the person or team that comes the closest to predicting their own course completion time for the activity they choose.

Hiking, biking, and walking strolls are ideal for those who enjoy nature. The entire family can participate in these activities that are designed for holding conversations. Ranger or self led tours, site-seeing tours, campfires, and picnicking are also excellent opportunities to get to know each other.

Museums, attractions, parks, monuments, family homesteads, former schools, and other off-site tours will complement the reunion itinerary. Event coordinators at locations that encourage reunions can offer a bevy of suggestions. If the site is not in the immediate vicinity, check with the local Convention and Visitors Bureau (CVB). They offer free materials and information on places to hold reunions. Besides area accommodations, they provide details on transportation, attractions, events, entertainment, and ancillary services such as florists, caterers, and off-site tours. Many CVBs are membership organizations, however, and must represent their affiliates equally.

Indoor Activities

Ask family members to bring charade topics, cards, bingo board games, checkers, dominoes, puzzles, and art projects. All these games allow for multi-age interactions and all help to stimulate familial connections. Musical instruments such as guitars, banjos, violins, flutes, clarinets, and harmonicas travel easily. The talented musicians in the group can play while others can join by singing and dancing. Bring some instruments that everyone could play: tambourines, kazoos, bamboo sticks, bongo drums, bells, and triangles.

Evening Activities

Ask people to bring home movies or videos and spend an evening sharing photos, slides, and albums. What other audience is there that will *truly* enjoy watching these home creations?

Plan a talent night where everyone can share their artistic forte. This could involve playing musical instruments, performing skits, singing, and dancing. Hire a band or DJ for one night when everyone can dress up and dance. This might be an opportunity to let the young ones have a separate evening to themselves with a pizza party and their favorite music on CDs.

Activities and tours needn't be structured every minute. Allow free time for families to plan their own activities and side trips.

Photography

Bring videos and shoot several photos. If a professional videographer is hired, family members won't have to risk missing part of the reunion. Also, a more professional product will result.

Ask a family member or hire a professional photographer. With a wide-angle lens, take several group photos. Even if a professional is brought in for one day, it will be a quality pictorial documentation of the reunion. Prearrange a time so everyone knows when photo sessions will take place and can plan their schedules and clothing accordingly. With groups of 50 or more, try to allow 45 minutes to an hour for the set up and shoot.

Of course, the cameras on smart-phones produce quality photos and videos and can contribute to the recording of the event. Set up a **Facebook, Twitter, Vimeo**, or **Instagram** page so everyone can upload their photos and recordings for all to view after the reunion.

Games and Contests
Think of games and contests that will entertain and provide information. These two games will promote learning about the family:

- Ask guests to send in family trivia questions or baby pictures before the reunion. One evening, play charades by forming family teams. Each team tries to answer family trivia or guess the identity of the baby pictures. Questions could be milestone dates or events, occupations, or the source of interesting life stories.
- Ask everyone to anonymously write down 6-10 interesting attributes about themselves or their likes and dislikes on a sheet of paper. Put the papers in a bowl and let each person pick one. The winners are the ones who guess the correct family member using the fewest clues.

Ticket Price
After all activities are planned and expenses are factored in, determine a ticket price. Mention all costs that go into the ticket price in the announcements. Remember, it probably won't be well received to plea for help in covering shortfalls at the reunion.

Family Souvenirs, Awards, and Prizes
T-shirts, Caps, Sweatshirts

T-shirts are the most common family reunion souvenir. They are inexpensive and can be worn by everyone. Add a family photo or family tree with the names of everyone who will attend the reunion. If t-shirts are ordered and paid for ahead of time, they can be worn at the reunion. To help identify family lineages, choose colors that represent each family branch. Hats, caps, and sweatshirts are also popular souvenirs.

Family Cookbook

A family cookbook is not only a memorable souvenir, it is a lifelong keepsake that won't go out of date or lose relevance. It usually represents a loving tribute to the family and can serve as a historical document for future generations.

Cookbooks are easy to put together, especially on a computer. Have people either email or take a picture of the hand written version which can be scanned into the cookbook. There also are websites that will organize it for you (some example websites are listed below). Otherwise, retype the recipes in a consistent format. A printer or copy shop can assemble the books. A combed or spiral binding is recommended since they wear well over time. The cover can display a picture from a prior reunion, a family member who is being honored or other historical snapshot.

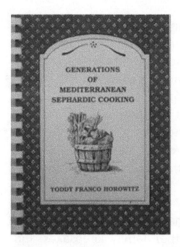

In order to add distinctiveness, place the person's picture next to their recipe.

If the budget allows, have cookbooks professionally assembled. There are many websites that can produce family cookbooks. Alternatively, keep it online so everyone can access it without having a physical book. Even if the cookbook is never printed, having online access to the family recipes means the family cookbook is only a mouse click away and recipes can be easily downloaded or emailed. These websites offer pre-designed covers that can be customized or created on your own.

Here are a few websites that describe how to assemble a family cookbook:

- http://familycookbookproject.com
- http://heritagecookbook.com
- http://morriscookbooks.com
- http://bookemon.com

Family Quilts

Family quilts are unique renditions of a family history. They are invaluable heirlooms that can be created and assembled at reunions and passed down through generations. Quilts usually represent the combined endeavors of many branches of the family and preserve events, experiences, and people. They can be created as one group project, or if enough squares are supplied, made in multiples so every family has one.

A reunion is an opportunity to bring patches or squares that reflect each family's personal traditions. Squares can be embroidered, drawn, cross-stitched, or sewn. Pictures can be scanned into computers and imprinted directly onto cloth. Comprise patches of a baby's blanket, one of grandmas' embroidered tablecloths or pillow cases, an aunt's dress, sports emblems, and a piece of a cousin's wedding gown.

Quilts can be auctioned at the reunion as a fundraiser or brought to each reunion as an heirloom display. Quilts can be immortalized by converting them onto stationery, puzzles, posters, and postcards which can also be available at the reunion.

Mementos

Additional mementos such as personalized wine bottles, pens, wine glasses, cups, key rings, and other family keepsakes and souvenirs can be used for awards or as fundraising items.

Family members could donate handcrafted items for door prizes and awards. Request donations in all mailings. Once they are in hand, give credit to the donors in future mailings and on display at the reunion.

Glassware, cups, bumper stickers, tote bags, coasters, paperweights, and pennants are all popular family reunion keepsakes and can be ordered in assorted amounts. The larger the order, the lower per unit cost.

Another activity that can also yield a memorable souvenir is to hire an artist to draw caricatures of each family group. It shouldn't be very expensive and will be a fun exercise.

Family Award Categories
- Oldest and youngest family member at the reunion
- Oldest and most recent married couple
- Newest parent or grandparent
- Youngest grandparent
- Most children, grandchildren, and great grandchildren
- Largest family unit present
- Family that has attended the most reunions

- Two family members that most look alike
- Oldest to retire or oldest still working
- Most descendants

Prizes

An advantage of door prizes and award donations is that they don't come out of the reunion budget. They might even have greater sentimental value. T-shirts, history books, or the family cookbook can also be used for awards.

Consider prizes that coincide with the award that is being presented:

- Oldest and youngest family members at the reunion: *a frame later to be filled with a picture taken of the two at the reunion*
- Newest married couple: *the family cookbook*
- Newest parent and/or grandparent: *frame with a photo of both families*
- Most children: *free babysitting at reunion by family members*
- Largest family unit present: *see if someone in the family will donate earned flight mileage*
- A family member that has attended the most reunions: *complementary tickets to the next reunion*

Displays

Besides quilts, hand made auction items, photo albums, a family tree, cookbook, heirlooms, and other memorabilia, there are several other items that can easily be used as display pieces.

Wine bottles with personalized labels like the one shown below from Windsor Vineyards can also serve as door prizes, souvenirs, or a fundraiser item.

Selected Especially To Celebrate
The Carniglia Family's
Annual Spring Fling

1999
NORTH COAST
CABERNET SAUVIGNON
Vintner's Reserve

Family Reunion Fundraising Ideas

There are several ways to cover reunion expenses, pay for scholarships, or supplement a family member's expenses.

- Add a small amount to the registration fee. This is the simplest method of raising extra cash. Everyone should understand that the ticket fee covers expenses. A slight mark up reduces the need to rely on reunion merchandise sales.

- Besides selling specially ordered items, handmade donations like quilts, paintings, tablecloths, pillows, or other handicrafts can be auctioned to the highest bidder. Encourage donations even from those who can't attend the reunion. If the object doesn't sell beforehand, hold a silent or live auction at the reunion. Homemade baked goods can also be brought to and sold at the reunion.

- If the reunion and the attendees are mostly local, purchase gift certificates from your favorite hair salons, movie theaters, restaurants, and specialty shops. They may even donate or offer a reduced price for your group. It never hurts to ask. Offer these as auction items in early mailers and have them available at the reunion for continued bidding.

- Group photos taken at the reunion. Collect money, including postage costs, and send out later.

- Create calendars with family pictures. Ask family members to send in photos. Combine several photographs in a collage format or use individual family pictures. There are many websites that can create them with the photos you provide. Order these well before the reunion, check production and delivery times.

11. Military Reunion Essentials

Soldiers share a unique bond. To many of those who served in the military, a common thread is that the friendships forged and the time involved was the strongest and most influential of their lives. They formed bonds under unusual conditions and the camaraderie lasts a life time.

The emotional attachments can be very strong. Organizers are typically retired personnel who plan regular reunions. They might even belong to several squadrons or units and attend frequent reunions. Therefore, they have become quite resourceful at organizing these events.

Many veterans want to preserve and support patriotic affiliations by organizing support groups through veterans' societies or hospitals. Veterans groups sponsor events and programs organizing daytime tours of local historical sites and national monuments. **http://www.vetfriends.com** is a national directory of military and veteran organizations in the United States and lists reunion information and a calendar of events that have been registered for the Army, Navy, Air Force, Marines, and Coast Guard. The site also allows members to search for veterans and military personnel among their online registry.

The American Legion lists reunions within a week of submittal on their website. Listings remain online until the day of the reunion, **http://www.legion.org/reunions**. For a reunion to be published in The American Legion Magazine, notices should be sent at least six months prior to the reunion. Because of the volume of reunions, a group's listing can only be placed once a year.

The Announcement

As mentioned earlier, make the invitations welcoming and enticing. If mailing out the invitations, personalize them to your unit. Check online for invitations that can be ordered or send announcements from websites that go out via email.

Sample Military Reunion Invitation

Military Reunion Venues

An important consideration for military reunion organizers is to find locations that come with practical financial savings. This could represent affordable hotels with nearby facilities or the ability to bring in liquor. Additional pluses of a free breakfast or hospitality room, free parking, or airport shuttles to and from the airport might also sweeten the pot. If families are included, it's helpful to find a location that has nearby activities, museums, and family friendly entertainment. Some ideas include:

- Historic military sites such as Norfolk (largest naval installation in the world), San Antonio (Alamo), San Diego (large naval base), Washington DC (all war monuments)
- Locations that have choices for various family activities such as Branson, Las Vegas, Amusement parks, and other family-oriented destinations

- Locations near battleships, air force bases, sky diving centers, marine bases, or army barracks
- Fort Bragg, Veterans Park in Fayetteville, North Carolina. **http://www2.visitfayettevillenc.com/military_in_cumbe rland_county/militaryreunions.html**
- **http://www.uniquevenues.com/military.** They list all kinds of unique venues for any event in various cities across the United States and Canada.

Battleship Reunions
A military reunion on a ship or battleground that made an impact on veterans' lives could be a healing aspect of the reunion. Battleship Massachusetts, for example, has reunions on their ship in Battleship Cove in Fall River, Maine. Call their Group Sales Manager 508.678.1100 ext: 101, or contact them through their website: **http://battleshipcove.org.** The only drawback is that ships might not be handicap accessible. Ships are often in their original configurations, so people in wheelchairs would need assistance to come up the gangway. Battleships Crewmates of the BB-59 come together for reunions of the battleship every year in June. It is the longest continual reunion in U.S. Navy history.

Air Force Reunions
Reunions held on or near an air force base are distinctive locations, especially if there are museums, events, and other activities nearby. The National Museum of the U.S. Air Force in Wright-Patterson AFB, Ohio, for example, hosts hundreds of reunion groups at the museum every year. The museum is a self-touring facility where groups can tour aircraft and exhibits. Contact their special events coordinator at 937.255.1712 or visit their website: **http://nationalmuseum.af.mil** where they list upcoming reunions.

There are also organizations, such as the Armed Forces Reunions, that plan military reunions for WWII, Korean War, and Vietnam War veterans' associations. Check their website or call for more information. **http://armedforcesreunions.com** or 800.562.7226.

Military Mementos

Special mementos might include a collection of writings, poems, letters, and stories of wartime experiences. Consolidate them into a booklet. Add period-related photographs and write tributes to those who have passed away. Related military books, monogrammed caps, t-shirts, paintings, and nostalgic photographs are also popular and reliable fundraising items.

Name tag buttons are also memorable and useful souvenirs. They can be customized to any military division and designed to be reused for multiple reunion events.

Get the Word Out

Contact national veterans' organizations that publish periodic magazines. They devote sections to upcoming military reunions. The American Legion, VFW, Forty and Eight Chateaus, Veterans Clubs, unit newspapers, local papers, membership rosters, and Veterans Magazines (the internet or libraries have lists of organizations and addresses) are just a few. Each issue of **Reunions Magazine** lists military reunion notices in their *Reunion Reveille.*

There are many websites related to specific military divisions that also announce reunions.

Three Months before the Reunion

75%

12. Countdown

Continue the phone drive, emails, group phone texts, posts on Facebook, or other outlet media concentrating on encouraging people to attend the reunion. Many don't make decisions until the bitter end, but with enough pressure, the hope is they realize what they would miss, not about what they might fear.

Name Tags
The phone drive should be continuing even this close to the event. Some folks still may not have heard about the reunion. However, there should be a substantial list of paid guests by now. If the committee is making the name tags begin with those who have paid so far.

Print Name Tags
 ✓ Print the list of 'Paid' guests for the name tags.
 ✓ Purchase the specified Avery Name Tag labels and either print directly on the tags or transfer the names onto the tags later.
 ✓ To save space, use only the women's maiden names. (For class reunions) for guest names of alumni, print the alumni's name (in smaller letters somewhere on the badge)

It is quite common to receive an influx of ticket payments days before the reunion. So that it isn't overwhelming right before the reunion, create tags for early registrants as soon as possible ahead of time. It is even a good idea to make name tags for those who suggested probable attendance. If they don't show up, save the tags as evidence of no-shows when the final tallying takes place.

One Month before the Reunion
Programs
Printed Program
A printed program that describes reunion events can also be a nice souvenir. One can easily be created using a standard 8½ x 11 inch sheet of heavy paper stock, (24 lb. paper weight is best), and folded in half. Put the school logo, family crest, or military insignia on the cover along with the name, date, and place of the reunion. On the inside, describe the reunion itinerary and activities. Some of the following suggestions are also possible:

- Picture of the school, family, homestead, or military insignia
- comments sent in expressing appreciation to reunion committee members and other volunteers,
- names and/or picture of the reunion committee members,
- any special guests,
- acknowledgments to donors of door prizes and awards,
- results of any reunion questionnaire or survey,
- copies of the school hymn, motto or song.

The Spoken Program
Any verbal program typically works best as guests are finishing their meal, during dessert or before dancing or other activity begins. It may be the one time during the evening that everyone's attention is focused on one activity. Some reunion committees prefer not to take any time away from reminiscing and don't have a pre-set program. However, some sort of program is usually planned at most reunions, if only to make short announcements.

Keep the program short, punchy, and focused. The keyword here is **short**. Long speeches are **not** recommended, unless they are brief remarks from invited teachers or guests. Long orations are not necessary or desired at reunions if reminiscing is the focus. Keep any visual portion of the program at a minimum as well.

A DJ or band leader can act as the master of ceremonies if necessary. Discuss this job with the entertainer before the reunion. If a committee member controls the program, make sure a podium and microphone are available. Hotels and restaurants usually provide these items at no additional charge.

Announcements

Provide any information on ancillary reunion events. If applicable, remind guests to get their pictures taken, purchase raffle tickets, help with the next reunion, send in address changes, or read any special letters or telegrams.

Acknowledgments, Introductions, and Presentations

Thank everyone individually who contributed to the planning of the reunion, donated door prizes, or went beyond the call of duty. Introduce any special guests and present any plaques or commemorations. If you don't have a professional photographer, ask someone to take still pictures of the special presentations for inclusion in the photo book or reunion album. Some suggestions for special presentations might be one or more of the following:

- Discuss any other planned reunion activities and events
- Suggest everyone wear name tags during all events
- Alumni came from (number of) different states to be here (fill in the number)
- Acknowledge any first time reunion attendees
- Introduce and thank committee members
- Introduce any honored or special guests
- Choose raffle tickets winners
- Announce award and/or any door prize winners

Awards

If awards will be given away for noteworthy achievements, begin a preliminary list. Reread the questionnaires and choose tentative award winners. As more responses arrive, winners of these awards may need to be revised. Past a certain age group, some award categories may not work. However, many can be appropriate for any type of reunion, such as:

- Married the longest
- Most recently married
- Traveled the furthest to the reunion
- Lives closest to the school, homestead or military base
- Most children, grandchildren
- Nearest to being a parent or grandparent
- First person to buy a reunion ticket
- Person who has attended the most reunions
- Most unique occupation
- Changed the least (this prize can be chosen the evening of the event with nominations during the program.)

There may be even more categories, but keep them tactful. For example, don't award a prize for "the least hair," "changed the most," or "married the most." The winner would probably not appreciate such recognition.

Door Prizes and/or Donations

Purchase any needed door prizes that require monograms or inscription. Items don't have to be expensive; attendees will appreciate any creative memento. If the committee is not designing their own tickets, double stubbed "movie tickets" are available in most party stores with matching numbers that can be used for selecting door prize winners or as raffle tickets. If door prizes are offered as services, present them on nicely designed coupons.

If anyone volunteered to provide prizes for goods or services, graciously acknowledge their donations. If applicable, remind them to bring the item to the reunion or make arrangements for items to be picked up ahead of time.

The First Impression Should be Inviting
Planning and setting up decorations and displays takes forethought, people power, and time management skills. Depending on how soon the banquet room is accessible, putting up elaborate decorations on the day of the reunion may be impossible. Consider the time available and plan accordingly.

If anyone on the committee is artistic, solicit their help in making welcome and informational signs for the registration area. Time permitting, include a picture or drawing of the school mascot, family crest, or military logo. Some example signs might include:

- Prepaid Tickets
- Will Call Tickets
- Reunion Items for Sale
- Raffle Tickets
- Drink Tickets
- Photos Taken Here
- Name Tags

Any displays, banners, or wall hangings must be removed at the end of the evening. Table centerpieces can be offered to the guests, but someone from the committee should be responsible for collecting all other decorations and memorabilia. A very reliable person needs to be in charge of the cash box. If the reunion is at a hotel, restaurant, or museum, ask the manager to lock the cash box in a safe deposit box once the registration tables close.

13. Final Arrangements

Two Weeks before the Reunion
During the final two weeks before the event, besides updating the guest list, making name tags, handouts, and other displays, the registration packets can be assembled. At this point, there should be plenty of registrants to begin this process. Begin putting together the packets as soon as possible because you will very likely be finishing them right up to the last minute.

The Guest List
Prepare a preliminary list of paid guests with names of all attendees, the number in each family unit, and the amounts paid. This list is essential for the registration tables. Since ticket payments will trickle in at the last minute, the final attendee list can be printed the day before or day of the reunion.

Print Attending Guest List
✓ Print a summary list of all paid attendees and their guests. This list includes each attendee's name, their guest name/s, phone number, and total paid.

Loose Ends
The following tasks should be ready or near completion:
- Handmade signs
- Decorations and table centerpieces
- Remind donors to bring door prizes. Have an extra bottle of wine on hand in case someone forgets to bring their donation.
- Confirm with those working the registration table, make notes listing their responsibilities
- Floral arrangements

- Check the attendance and arrival time for all vendors:
- The entertainer. Verify the DJ or band leader has your song list and will play **the** *designated* selections
- Photographer
- Videographer
- T-shirts and others

Finally, check that invited guests have the reunion time and location information and arrange for their hotel rooms, if applicable. If the budget allows, offer to pay for their hotel room if they are planning to spend the night.

Make sure there are options for people not to drink and drive. This can involve the availability of taxis, LYFT on-demand ride sharing, **http://lyft.me**, or designated drivers. Also, recommend using car pools. If the reunion is being held at a different location than the hotel guests are staying at, ask if the hotel offers a van service.

Memory Album, Handouts, and Displays
Two weeks should be the deadline for making changes to anything going to a printer. Deliver a camera-ready draft of the memory album, family history chronicle, program, t-shirt, or other handout to the printer or vendor. Allow sufficient time to receive the final product before the reunion. Waiting until this last acceptable date enables you include any last minute submissions. Always allow extra time for the delivery of the final product because unforeseen delays always occur. Allow several hours for final proofreading, Check the spelling of names.

The banner, posters, displays, and prizes should be in hand by now. If there is a slide show or video presentation, go through a rehearsal to verify that the slides are in proper order and show time is kept to the designated time frame. (Remember, the entire program should not last more than 10 – 15 minutes.)

Mail Tickets

If using physical tickets, it is recommended to not wait later than two weeks before the reunion to mail them out, first class of course. The U.S. mail system can be unpredictable, so don't take the risk of tickets not being received on time. If tickets or confirmations were emailed or confirmed online, remind guests to bring their printed verifications to the reunion.

Print Address Labels if Mailing Tickets
- ✓ Print address labels for all paid guests.
- ✓ Purchase ample postage and envelopes for the ticket mailing

If sending out tickets, emails, or even posting announcements on the reunion webpage or Facebook group page, include the reunion itinerary again. This will also be useful for those who indicated they will be attending other reunion-related activities.

One Week before the Reunion
Registration Packets
If professional planners are organizing the reunion, they will handle the entire check-in process, so you can skip this section.

After updating the guest list with any last minute ticket purchases, prepare an updated attendance list. Based on the contents of the registration packet, use appropriately sized envelopes. Three or four people can stuff the packets in a few hours.

Indicate the guests names (last name first) and the number of paid tickets on the outside of each envelope. If any guests owe a balance, or will pay at the door, highlight the **"Balance Due $_____"** in red on the envelope. (See sample below.) These envelopes should be at the Will Call table. This conspicuous reminder will help the person collecting payments save time.

SMITH, (Hunter) Sally & Roger 2

BALANCE DUE -- $50.00

Name Tags, Buttons, or Other ID
Include names for the spouses and guests of the main person for class and military reunions. For family reunions, as an alternative to pre-made name tags, guests can create their own as a craft activity.

Prepare extra registration packets for those who said they might attend (hold these at the Will Call section). It won't take much extra effort and the packets will be ready when and if they show up.

Refunds or Prepaid Purchase Items
Insert any refunds that may be due in the packets. Along with the packets, check-in workers can hand out any reunion souvenirs that were part of the ticket price: class directory, a memory album, video, CD, etc.

If tickets were mailed out and some people paid too late to have their tickets sent to them, place these prepaid tickets in their packets.

Registration Table
A smooth-operating registration process is essential. No one wants to spend a lot of time checking in. Once people start to see familiar faces, they'll want to start talking. Therefore, the check-in process needs to be quick and painless. Everyone will appreciate it. Have the following items available:

- Alphabetized Registration Packets

- An alphabetical list of all prepaid attendees with number of guests and amounts paid
- List of Will Call guests
- Any prepared reunion programs, goody bags, souvenirs, memory albums, family history books, and/or other hand outs
- To reduce check-in time even further, prepare large block letters in two or three alphabetical sections. For example, if 200 or more people are attending, depending upon the available space and number of registration volunteers, try forming three lines such as: **A - H, I - R** and **S - Z.**

Quick Tip: *Ask if the facility has stands to display these signs behind each letter grouping.*

- Blank name tags or buttons and someone with good handwriting skills to make them on the spot
- Pens, pencils, blank envelopes, tape, paper clips, scissors, stapler, and staples

- A cash box with change including some one, five, and ten dollar bills for the Will Call table and raffle ticket purchases
- Door prize tickets
- A wastepaper basket
- Container for raffle tickets and/or door prize ticket stubs

Quick Tip: *Use three rolls of ticket stubs in different colors. For example: blue for the dinner tickets, red for raffle tickets, and orange for door prizes. Put stubs for each drawing into separate containers.*

Final Meeting Agenda
- Stuff registration envelopes
- Create any last minute name tags or signs
- Update any new award winner changes (such as who came the furthest to the reunion)

Go over all the event details with the committee so everyone understands the timing and general flow of the event

Reunion Day Assignments
Assemble enough volunteers to handle all tasks. Depending upon the amount of guests expected, assign tasks accordingly. For example, a reunion of 150 or more might look like this:

Set up:	2:00 - 5:00pm	3-5 people
Registration tables	6:00 - 8:00pm	3-5 people
Will call/Sales	6:00 - 8:00pm	1-2 people
Clean up:	Everyone available	

Check-in Responsibilities
Besides cheerfully greeting people, registration workers will be in charge of the following:

- Handing out registration packets, any prepaid items as memory albums, programs or other prepared booklets. (Alternatively, place programs at each place setting.)

- Direct guests toward the photographer to have their pictures taken. (The photographer should confirm pictures are taken without name tags.)
- If there are door prize tickets, separate the tickets and put stubs in a container or bowl for the later drawing.

To promote an orderly reception process with the least amount of waiting time, delegate assignments. Explain them again while they are sitting with the information in front of them.

If registrations workers are guests of the function, assign only one-hour shifts and plan for a second shift. If spouses of alumni are helping, they can probably work the entire entry process. Check-in tables needn't be manned for the entire event. **Those who arrive after dinner should be charged part of the ticket price since there are many other costs associated with the reunion besides the meal.** Decide on and charge a fee for those who show up after dinner. (Mention this cost in all mailings.)

Getting guests to work the check-in tables when they are anxious to join in the festivities will be difficult. It's best if family members (who are paying guests) handle the registration tables. Otherwise, the committee may have to hire workers and provide each a meal, which could be costly. The facility may have its own guards to monitor the area. Unfortunately, they won't be noticing late arrivals that look like they belong there.

Will Call
Will Call transactions should be handled separately from the prepaid registrants. This will greatly reduce confusion and waiting time at the check-in tables. Cash and credit card settlements take longer. This separate system enables those handling payment transactions to concentrate on just that. With two people, they can manage all cash sales, including raffle tickets and other purchases.

If unreserved guests show up at the door, the registration workers should place their payments inside an envelope and indicate the purchaser's name on the envelope. It is **especially important to identify guests who pay with cash.** Accounting for unidentified cash ticket payments after the reunion can be very frustrating. **The cash box should always be under supervision or in a safe place throughout the reunion.**

If credit card purchases are accepted and there is a concern the committee shouldn't incur any more expenses, add in the additional 3% credit card fee to their tab or 5% for Pay Pal accounts.

Meal Count
The catering manager will require a meal count guarantee before the event and may even want full payment a week prior. In addition to the confirmed guests, estimate a few more who said they would pay at the door. Most restaurant facilities can accommodate up to a 7% overage of the guarantee (check with the facility) for unexpected guests.

There is no need to overestimate the number of unexpected arrivals because the inevitable no-shows will usually balance the few unannounced guests. Refunds are not usually requested, or for that matter, offered at reunions. The time, effort, and additional cost factors that reunion committees incur more than compensate for paid no-shows. Nevertheless, if there is an emergency or enough notice is received, try to accommodate those guests with some amount.

Work out a diagram of how the tables should be set up including the registration tables so there will be no confusion or lengthy discussions during the reunion. (Sample diagram on next page.) It will be very helpful to have such details worked out in advance to avoid any potential last minute problems or surprises. This diagram will also be helpful for the management and meal caterer. If an off-site caterer has been hired, a prepared layout will be practical in advance of the reunion.

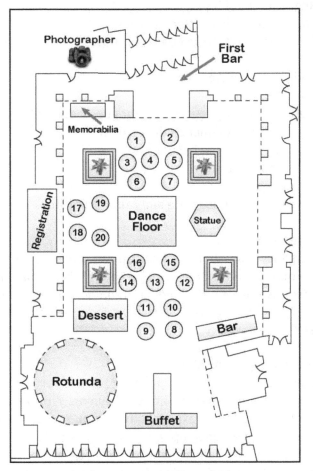

Sample room layout with seating for 200 people

Equipment

Confirm availability of the following items with the reunion facility. Hopefully, when negotiating the contract, you were able to get much of the following equipment included in the overall fee. Any additional costs should already be accounted for in the budget. However, it's wise to verify with the facility that any other items will be available.

- Registration tables
- Stands for holding letters or signs
- Easels and/or bulletin boards for posters, pictures, and other displays
- Podium and microphone
- Dance floor
- Plenty of water pitchers (so your guests don't always have to pay for drinks to quench their thirst)
- A place to hang the banner
- Screen for slide show
- A/V equipment
- Containers for door prize and raffle ticket stubs

Staff Contingency Plan

An emergency plan should be set up for someone to take over decision making and overall management of the reunion in case a key person is unable to attend the reunion. At least one other person should be aware of the evening's responsibilities and prepared to take over.

If Finances are Running Short

As stated earlier, it is bad practice to ask for assistance in defraying reunion expenses at the reunion. Hopefully, good budgeting ensured that expenses have not exceeded revenues and enough people signed up to cover the costs. However, in the event finances are running short, refer to some suggestions described in Chapter 5, under 'Fundraising Ideas,' for ideas on raising some last minute cash.

If a shortage occurs at a family reunion, a last minute appeal on the reunion website or an email notice sent to the group may bring in enough funds to cover any short fall.

The Reunion Event

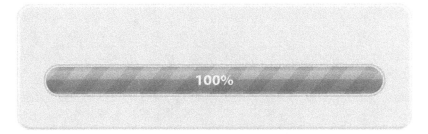

100%

14. Reunion Day

The moment everyone has been waiting for has finally arrived! This chapter provides scenarios and approximate time frames for reunion-related events.

Make sure committee members know their expected arrival time and when to be available for the committee picture. Allow extra time to set up the banquet room. Bring any reunion attire if there is no time to return home.

Reunion Day Check List
Copy the list on the following page or go to our website and print off the **Reunion Day Checklist**. Check off the items as they are handled.

Print Event Day Check List
> ✓ Under Checklists, print Event-Day Check List.

CHECKLIST

Items to Bring		Things to Do	
Registration packets		Set up table centerpieces	
Memory albums, programs		Set up decorations, posters	
Cash Box		Set up registration area	
Guest List with Payment Status		Hang banners, posters, etc.	
Cell phone or computer with Calculator		Arrange check-in packets alphabetically	
Signs for reception area and elsewhere		Reserve strategic seat or table for committee members	
Memorabilia, photo collage, other displays		Meet with and go over duties with registration desk workers	
Blank name tags for late arrivals		Take committee pictures before reunion begins	
Stapler, Scotch Tape		Confirm meal arrangements and serving time frame with catering manager	
Sharpies, Pens and Pencils		Confirm song list with DJ	
Banner , posters, other decor		ENJOY ALL THAT HAS BEEN PLANNED	
Table Centerpieces			
Door Prizes			
Awards or Certificates			
Receipt book and Checkbook			
Program Notes			
Smart phone w/ camera/video			
Reunion Clothes (if necessary)			

Optional or as Needed

Easels and Bulletin Boards.	
TVs, screens and other video equipment	
Extension cords	

A scenario on how a typical class reunion weekend is outlined below. Family and military reunions may have more events and activities throughout based on the number of days of the reunion and size of the group.

FRIDAY NIGHT

> Opening reception in hospitality suite.................7:00 pm
> Introductory activities..8:00 pm
> Games or other ice-breaker..............................9:00 pm

SATURDAY

> Evening activities..6:30 – 11 pm
> (Detailed below)

Evening Banquet

- Take group committee picture and their family portraits before guests arrive.

> Social time... 6:30 - 8:00 pm
> Dinner.. 8:00 - 9:30 pm
> Program.. 9:10 - 9:30 pm
> Dancing and Reminiscing .... 9:30 pm --?

At the Facility

- Set up table centerpieces, posters, decorations, and banners
- Organize check-in tables with alphabetized registration packets
- Discuss the evening's agenda with catering manager, photographer, and entertainer.
- Clarify with the entertainer his or her role in the evening, i.e. if they will act as a Master of Ceremonies or just provide music. Decide if they should honor any song requests made by guests. Remind them to keep the music level *low*, especially during the reminiscing part of the evening, and if the volume should be adjusted for dancing. (After all, this is *your* reunion. Insist on this.)
- Verify how late the photographer will be available to take portrait pictures and still take candid shots of the reunion.

- Go over responsibilities and time commitments with registration desk workers.

Program Agenda
Refer to the program agenda discussed in Chapter 12, *Countdown*, and have fun.

Before Leaving the Event
- Retrieve cash box, banner, posters, registration supplies, and memorabilia
- Pay facility or caterer any contract balance due

SUNDAY
    Brunch or picnic .... 11:00 am – 2 pm

Additional Events

Having more than one reunion event presents an opportunity for people to bring their families and continue reminiscing. It also allows many who were unable to attend the dinner-dance a chance to participate in another activity.

If the cost of a Sunday meal was not included in the original ticket price, and a picnic is planned, remind people to bring their own food and sports equipment. Items for the committee to bring:

- Banner
- Lunch or snacks
- Memory books and other souvenirs for new arrivals
- Reunion sale items and receipt book
- Smart phone with camera (for more pictures for the photo book or memory album)

15. Wrap Up

Congratulations on completing a milestone event! Except for a few loose ends, consider this masterful job done.

Closing Costs
The only financial liability remaining, besides reimbursements to committee members for any personal monies they had to front, should be the final payment to the photographer for the preparation and mailing of the photo albums. Payment will probably be required at the time the paste up of the photo album is delivered.

Update the Reunion Website
While everyone is still energized by event, keep the ambiance alive by placing photos of the reunion on your group's website where people can add their own and comment. It's great fun to relive the event while memories are still fresh. Otherwise, use an online photo album like **http://www.shutterfly.com** or a Facebook Group page to post an album of event photos.

Memory Album or Photo Book
This project should be completed as soon as possible. Everyone will appreciate receiving the booklet with names and contact information while experiencing the reunion afterglow and attendees can quickly follow up on contacts made at the reunion.

The photographer should send the book proof within a few weeks after the reunion with instructions on what is needed. Upon receipt, the committee should verify all name spellings and match ups to the right photos.

If the committee is creating the photo book, custom-design a cover using any word processing software. Insert the group's logo or picture identifier and include the details of the event.

Introductory Page

- Brief statement thanking everyone who attended the reunion and why it was so successful.
- Reunion facts: name, date, and place of reunion
- Picture of school, class insignia, family crest, or military logo
- List of award winners, such as "Who Traveled the Farthest to the Reunion?"
- Names of committee members
- A memorial page
- Contact information for future reunions
- Roster or directory of names and addresses.

Print Roster for Memory Book

✓ Print the entire roster with the group's names and addresses in a small font so as not to use up several pages of the photo book.

Collage Pages

If making your own photo books, several software programs, such as Photoshop, are perfect for inserting photos and arranging them on each page. It is also very helpful to add names (especially maiden names) on or near each guest's photo. If professional photographers are preparing the booklets, see if you can arrange your own collage pages for insertion into their product. It's less work for them, and it will be a better photo book for your group since some people may not be recognizable.

Thank You Notes

Send thank you notes to special guests, the facility event coordinator, the reunion coordinator of the school, committee members who volunteered their time, those who donated services or prizes, and others deserving appreciation.

Sample Memory Album or Photo Book Cover

Remaining Memory Albums or Photo Books
Send memory albums and/or photo books to anyone who purchased them separately. Also, send books to those who paid to attend the reunion but didn't show up.

Follow-up Letter, Email, or Online Post
A follow up letter, email, or website post shortly after the reunion can accomplish several goals:

- Extends the positive energy of the reunion
- Stimulates on-going connections
- Reminds members to keep the committee informed of any contact information updates
- Raises additional funds by providing one last chance to purchase any reunion items

If the letter goes out before the photo book or memory album is ready, business card ads can still be solicited. Other items could be sold to those who missed the event or who didn't buy them at the reunion. A sample note is shown next:

Dear Fellow Patriots:

Based on feedback so far, our recent reunion was such a great success, we can't wait for the next one. Don't worry; it's not too late to order any of the following items:

Reunion Video: If you missed the reunion or would like to order the professional video of the reunion event, the cost is $35, including shipping. The company who filmed the event is editing it now. It will be complete in about six weeks.

Photo Book: The memory album or photo book is also in preparation and should be completed and sent in about 8 weeks. There is still time to advertise business cards in the booklet. The cost of a business card ad is $15. Deadline is Oct. 25th. For those who did not attend the reunion, the photo book that includes a directory is $20.00.

Address Changes. Much of our time planning reunions is spent finding people. Please keep us posted with any contact information changes.

Please write checks out to the Reunion Committee and mail to: Jane Doe, 12345 East Lane, Lakewood, CO 80228. (303) 555-1212

Name_____Hm Ph_____

Address_____Bus Ph_____

_____ Email_____

$_____Add the enclosed business card in the Photo Book: $15

$_____Reunion Video: $35

$_____ Reunion Photo Book: $20

$_____TOTAL ENCLOSED

Close the Book on this Reunion
Bank Account
Upon completion of the reunion, prepare a budget review. If possible, do this the day after the reunion. Add up any receipts from the reunion event and formulate a final tally of revenues and expenses including costs yet to be paid, such as the photo book.

The reunion bank checking account can be closed after all bills have been paid and checks have cleared. If everything was budgeted carefully, a balance should remain. Open up a no-fee savings account and either keep any surplus for the next reunion or if this is a class reunion, consider donating part of the surplus to your school in honor of your class. This small deed gives back something in return for what the school meant to the class.

If there is a reunion website, encourage attendees to post their photos or videos from the reunion. Many will post comments on the reunion as well. Create a survey and ask attendees to indicate what they liked or any suggestions for future reunions.

Storage of Supplies
Back up all reunion data on another medium other than the computer that stores the existing information. Put all remaining supplies, photo books, name tags, and memorabilia in a storage box. This will be very helpful for the next reunion, no matter who plans it.

Maintain Connections
- Periodically update the reunion website with pictures and announcements
- Organize mini reunions between the main ones

Reflect and Revise

In the next few weeks, while everything is still fresh in your mind, have a wrap up party at someone's home or other meeting area. Make it a festive committee gathering where the committee can relax, reflect, and revise. Have a potluck meal and show the reunion video. Everyone will be busy reminiscing about the reunion, so this will be an opportunity to collect more ideas.

Ask everyone to present their thoughts on what worked and what didn't and if they have suggestions for improvements on any aspect of the event, for example:

- Satisfaction with venue
- Timing of the event
- Reception process
- Audio or spoken program changes
- Larger reception area
- Dining area configuration changes
- Dancing area needs
- Sound system adequacy
- Overall flow of the event

The Post Reunion Blues

Inevitably, post reunion let-down ensues. A cure for maintaining camaraderie is to continue with periodic, casual mini reunions. This ongoing contact will help sustain connections. Keep the reunion webpage, or Facebook group page, current with ongoing pictures, stories, and updates of interest to the group. Such efforts should encourage interaction, at least until the next reunion is in the works.

16. After the Reunion

Now that the reunion is over, don't let the excitement and enthusiasm dissipate. Stay up to date with reunion planning by checking our website and others on the internet and online book stores for updates and new ideas. Besides the reunion related websites mentioned throughout this book, more associations and related support services will open up.

If your event was successful, everyone will be looking forward to the next reunion. If the torch is passed along to someone else for the next reunion, lend support and information. If the same group initiates the next reunion, keep updated on the latest time saving techniques and developments.

If many believe the next reunion can't possibly surpass the previous one, don't believe it. With the experience and know how gained, the next reunion will be even better.

Stay in Touch between Reunions
By maintaining contact via a newsletter, reunion website, regular emails, or other correspondence, the contact lists that were so much work to create are maintained.

It is much easier to organize casual get-togethers between the larger events when having it at someone's home, restaurant, or park. Ask guests to pay for their own meals at the venue, bring their own, or have a pot-luck. Notices can be sent via email or posted on your reunion website or Facebook group page. Ask for an RSVP or post responses on the webpage.

Give us Feedback

Before the book is closed on the reunion, please share your expertise with other reunion planners. Please blog or post comments on our website in our Community Forum.

Please revisit our website, **http://reunionplanner.com**, for new ideas and shortcuts. In addition to our free reunion websites, we have more reunion-related resources, products, and services.

For questions or comments regarding anything in this book or the companion software, simply contact us through our website.

Remember that no matter what the economic climate, rain or shine, reunions will go on. They are distinct events that allow us to revisit special moments in our lives and become milestones themselves. We need the special handful of people like you who take the initiative to bring the rest of us together. Completing this process becomes rewarding beyond measure for everyone involved.

May your lives be blessed with many happy and financially successful reunions!

Sample Invitations and Questionnaires

Family Reunion

what

when

where

time

additional information

it's a REUNION!

what
It's a Celebration to
commemorate our 1987
Highschool graduation class!

date
January 25, 2011

time
4:00 PM - 9:00 PM

where
Beverly Hilton, Wilshire Blvd

additional info
Bring your families!

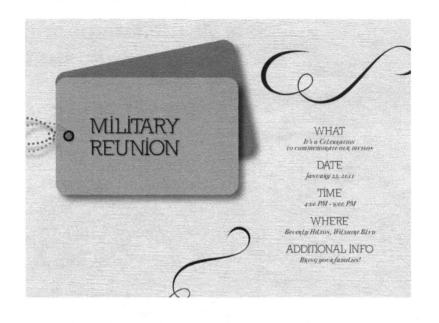

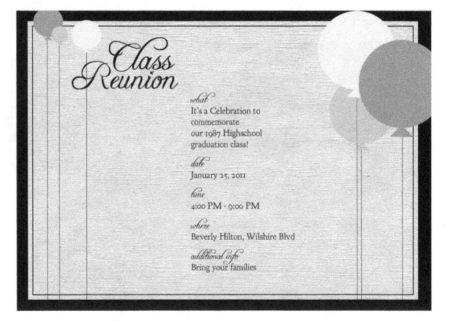

IT'S A REUNION!

what
A Company Reunion Party!

date
20 February 2011

time
11:00 AM - 5:00 PM

where
The Garden Patio

rsvp
Sara Saperstein

additional information
Casual Dress

MILITARY REUNION

WHAT
Join us for a
military gathering

DATE
30 March 2011

TIME
11:00 AM EST

WHERE
12345 army road
military city, usa

ADDITIONAL INFORMATION
add more info here

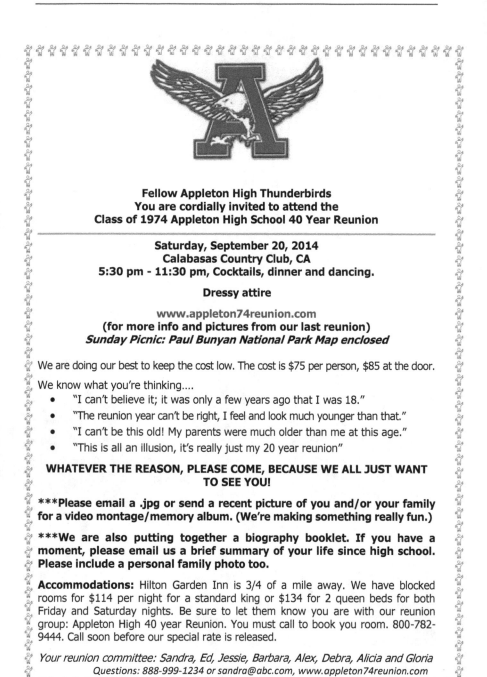

Fellow Appleton High Thunderbirds
You are cordially invited to attend the
Class of 1974 Appleton High School 40 Year Reunion

Saturday, September 20, 2014
Calabasas Country Club, CA
5:30 pm - 11:30 pm, Cocktails, dinner and dancing.

Dressy attire

www.appleton74reunion.com
(for more info and pictures from our last reunion)
Sunday Picnic: Paul Bunyan National Park Map enclosed

We are doing our best to keep the cost low. The cost is $75 per person, $85 at the door.

We know what you're thinking....

- "I can't believe it; it was only a few years ago that I was 18."
- "The reunion year can't be right, I feel and look much younger than that."
- "I can't be this old! My parents were much older than me at this age."
- "This is all an illusion, it's really just my 20 year reunion"

WHATEVER THE REASON, PLEASE COME, BECAUSE WE ALL JUST WANT TO SEE YOU!

***Please email a .jpg or send a recent picture of you and/or your family for a video montage/memory album. (We're making something really fun.)

***We are also putting together a biography booklet. If you have a moment, please email us a brief summary of your life since high school. Please include a personal family photo too.

Accommodations: Hilton Garden Inn is 3/4 of a mile away. We have blocked rooms for $114 per night for a standard king or $134 for 2 queen beds for both Friday and Saturday nights. Be sure to let them know you are with our reunion group: Appleton High 40 year Reunion. You must call to book you room. 800-782-9444. Call soon before our special rate is released.

Your reunion committee: Sandra, Ed, Jessie, Barbara, Alex, Debra, Alicia and Gloria
Questions: 888-999-1234 or sandra@abc.com, www.appleton74reunion.com

Return this page.

Not to fret, soon you'll be thinking: "This is a wake-up call; I need to get in better shape." Or, you could have one of the following reasons: "I had better go to this reunion because...

❑ What the heck, it's only 1 weekend out of the year.

❑ I am really looking forward to seeing my high school buds.

❑ I haven't seen _____ in many years. (Be sure to invite them!)

❑ What else is more important that I can't go to my reunion once every 10 years?

❑ I have never been to a reunion before, this should be fun.

❑ If this is the 40th, I sure don't want anyone to see me at our 50th.

❑ I am really looking forward to a fun event with people I haven't seen in a long time.

❑ While I have changed, so has everyone else. Now, I'm interested in hearing what they have done with their lives, who they have become and share a few laughs and fond memories about my old stomping grounds.

Let us know some of your favorite songs of our era. (Write on back if necessary)

_____

_____

Please call or let us know the whereabouts of any classmates. (Check the website for the missing persons list and email us if you have information on these classmates.)

_____

We want to see you all, talk to you, reminisce, laugh revisit old times, share funny stories and just have a fun time with some old friends, acquaintances, classmates or just some old people from the neighborhood.

We have much planned to make this the best reunion ever. Your attendance is the most important.

Tickets are $75 per person; $85 at the door.

Yes, I/we will be attending the 40th reunion! My information is below along with my check.

_____

Name: First, (Maiden) Last & Guest name   *Include Guest's name for badges!*

_____

Address

_____

City, State, Zip   Home / Cell Phone

_____

                                                    $ _____

Email   Amount enclosed

Please make checks out to: "Appleton High Class of 1974 Reunion"

Mail to: Bob Smith at 1234 First St., Los Angeles, CA 90010

DON'T MISS OUT...
Truman High School 20 Year Reunion

Thanksgiving Weekend, 2015

Marriott Hotel, Kansas City

5:30 pm - 11:30 pm, Cocktails, dinner and dancing.
Featuring musical highlights of our era.
Suggested Dress: Cocktail Attire

Tickets: $80 per person; $85 at the door. Prepaid tickets will be held at the door.

Register and purchase tickets on our class reunion website: www.TrumanHigh20YearReunion.com. Or, send check to "Truman Patriots Class of 1994" and mail to: Bob Lewis, 123 5th St., Kansas City, MO

We are putting together a biography /family photo booklet. Please email us a brief summary of your life since high school. Use some of the questions listed below as a guideline if you need inspiration. Please include a family photo in a jpg format.

1. If married, how long?
2. Number of children?
3. How many careers did you explore and were you satisfied with the path you took?
4. What would you do differently, if you knew then what you know now?
5. Was there a particular teacher in high school that that you especially admired?

Please call or let us know the whereabouts of any classmates. (See Missing Persons list enclosed or check the website and email us if you have information on anyone listed.)

- Cost of biography booklets is included in the ticket price. If you are not attending the reunion, the price is $20 including postage. Deadline for sending in biography and family photo is Nov 14, 2015 to be printed in time for the reunion.

- If you would like to include a business card in our post-reunion photo book, the cost is $10. Cards will be in the photo book to be sent after the reunion.

Please complete form below and send with a check for all purchases.

Name, First, (Maiden) Last & Guest name   *Include Guest's name for badges!*

Address

City, State, Zip   Home and Cell Phone
number

                                        $

Email   (very important)   Amount enclosed

Chi Omega Sorority
Homecoming Weekend
University of Wisconsin, Madison

Please join us for Alumni Weekend during Homecoming at UW
October 24 – 26, 2014

Follow us on Twitter @ChiOmegaNu

Post your pictures on Instagram:
http://instagram.com/wisalumni#

Friday Night October 24, 2014
Mixer at the Sorority House
6:00 – 9:00 pm

Saturday October 25, 2014
Football game: Wisconsin Badgers vs. Indiana Hoosiers
9:00 am – noon

Dinner at Madison Concourse Hotel & Governor's Club.
7pm – 11pm

Sunday October 26, 2014
Farewell Breakfast at the Sorority House
10:00 am

Email us and go on our website to make your reservations.

See the Alumnae Chapter Locator to find fellow UW Chi Omega alums and invite them to join us.

Help support our scholarship foundation.

ReunionPlanner.com
Make your Reunion a Social and Financial Success

Please come to our first Garvey Family Reunion

When: Friday, April 10, - Sunday, April 12, 2015
Where: Montesito Sequoia Lodge, Sequoia National Forest
Cost: $120 per family of 3, $175, families of 4. Contact lodge for available rooms.
Website: http://mslodge.com, 800.227.9900, reserve@mslodge.com

Schedule of Events

Friday Night: Evening get-together with hors d'oeuvres and dinner in the Marmot Lodge Meeting Room. Followed by family talent show around the campfire and s'mores.

Saturday Day: Choose your activity from canoeing, rock climbing, tennis, archery, arts and crafts, guided hikes, swimming in the lake, or just relax.

Saturday Night: Dinner in the Ponderosa Room followed by Karaoke Night.

Sunday Day: Picnic by the lake, farewell gathering in lobby.

Transportation: Call Sam Garvey for details.

Bring: Favorite stories, instruments for talent show, family pictures and handmade creation for door prizes. (If everyone brings something, everyone wins).

Make checks payable to and send to:
Sam Garvey, 123 Olive St., Palo Alto, CA 94301,
Questions: 713.973.0000

Reservation Form:
Our family will have ____ adults and ____ children in attendance
Name:_____
Address:_____
Phone and email:_____

Sample Budget Worksheet

ASSUMPTIONS	
Total Membership	
Estimated Turnout	
Estimated Family Unit (each guest unit @ 65%)	
Tables Required (10 people per table)	

ESTIMATED EXPENSES

Item	Unit	Item	Per Unit	Total
Meal (inc tax & tip)		person		
Entertainment				
Postage		env/2 mailings		
Printing / copying				
Name Tags		person		
Centerpieces		table		
Balloons / Decor				
Posters / Signs				
Programs/Memory Book		Family unit		
Door prizes / Awards		prize		
A/V Equipment				
Banner				
Souvenirs		person		
Insurance				
Miscellaneous				

TOTAL EXPENSES

ESTIMATED REVENUES

Item	Unit Amt.	Item	Per Unit	Tota
Ticket sales		person		
Item sales		item		
Advertising		ad		
Donations				

TOTAL REVENUES

REVENUES MINUS EXPENSES

COST PER PERSON

Website References

REUNION LOCATIONS, Military

REUNION PLANNERS

TRAVEL IDEAS

Index

W

Will call, 147, 148, 150, 151

Wine bottle inscriptions, 103, 129

Wineries and Vineyards, 40, 42, 103, 104, 129

Y

Yacht cruise, 39

Yearbooks, 47, 62, 78

CPSIA information can be obtained
at www.ICGtesting.com
Printed in the USA
LVHW03s1033080718
583079LV00008B/402/P